Creative Teaching for All

In the Box, Out of the Box, and Off the Walls

JACK ZEVIN

ROWMAN & LITTLEFIELD EDUCATION
A division of
ROWMAN & LITTLEFIELD PUBLISHERS, INC.
Lanham • New York • Toronto • Plymouth, UK

KH

Published by Rowman & Littlefield Education
A division of Rowman & Littlefield Publishers, Inc.
A wholly owned subsidiary of The Rowman & Littlefield Publishing Group, Inc.
4501 Forbes Boulevard, Suite 200, Lanham, Maryland 20706
www.rowman.com

10 Thornbury Road, Plymouth PL6 7PP, United Kingdom

British Library Cataloguing in Publication Information Available

Library of Congress Cataloging-in-Publication Data

Zevin, Jack.
  Creative teaching for all : in the box, out of the box, and off the walls / Jack Zevin.
      pages cm
  Includes bibliographical references.
  ISBN 978-1-61048-402-2 (cloth : alk. paper) — ISBN 978-1-61048-403-9 (pbk. : alk. paper) — ISBN 978-1-61048-404-6 (electronic) 1. Teaching. 2. Creative teaching.
I. Title.
  LB1025.3.Z465 2013
  371.107—dc23

                                                                2012050561

Printed in the United States of America

10/6/14

To all those seeking, finding, losing,
and rediscovering the creative spirit within.

IN THE BOX, OUT OF THE BOX, OFF THE WALLS

Secret ribbons,
palette's offer
the push
of a button,
minds on
shuffle
inside the
masquerade.

(Micah Zevin)

Contents

Acknowledgments

Creativity is heightened in my opinion by living a rich and varied life. "Variety is the spice of life," the old bromide goes, giving opportunities to try the new and innovative as well as cherish the old and familiar. New classes, new students, and new experiences have stimulated thinking about how teachers reach students through imagination and provocation instead of following predictable roles.

Therefore I wish to extend to my students, all teachers or teachers to be, my warmest appreciation for providing feedback about efforts to capture and engage them and their pupils. In the preparation of this book, particular gratitude is extended to my wife, Iris, who is (surprise!) a teacher and a sounding board for many ideas, both wacky and sound. Also, special thanks to another teacher, my consulting editor, Ms. Madelyn Roesch, who checked and rechecked my occasionally labyrinthine thinking and complicated prose.

But in creative teaching, questions, confusion, argument, and mystery often beat clarity.

FIGURE A.1
Triple spiral labyrinth (author)

Finally, a word of thanks to future readers, particularly teachers, who step outside the box and perhaps even go to the walls attempting to foster imagination and empathy rather than the usual bottom line of recitation, recall, and offering judgments from "on high."

Part I

CREATIVE TEACHING IN THE BOX, OUT OF THE BOX, AND OFF THE WALLS

INTRODUCTION

Creativity is often talked about in terms of "boxes" that limit thinking. The metaphor extends to many settings ranging from education to business, government, and the home. "Think outside the box" is practically on the order of saying, "have a nice day." It has become a standard phrase, almost a cliché.

"Off the walls" implies that we have managed to get outside the box of ordinary thinking and ideas are bouncing off the surfaces surrounding us. If only we can catch one. It also suggests a bit of madness.

Just what the box means, where outside is, and what makes up the walls is almost never discussed or dissected. This applies to ideas about home, school, and business. Most of us believe that we can think "outside" the usual ways, but that is really more difficult than it appears at first glance.

Most people view the box as a simile for containment, limiting our freedom to think in new or different ways. Going outside the box is an assumed solution, and it seems to be viewed as amenable to command. Go outside the box and solutions, ideas, actions will occur to you right away. Would that it could be so easy! If it were, we would all be brilliant. Most problems would be solved. We'd have almost nothing to do, just have fun.

However, as we all know, deep in our hearts, thinking outside the box is not easy. Outside may well put us in danger of ridicule or social opprobrium.

FIGURE I.1

Thinking outside the box implies that the folks surrounding us really want new ideas and solutions to problems, but that may not be true. They may actually be satisfied with the status quo, leaving things just as they are because that is the easiest road to follow. Or they may be afraid, even terrified, of new or unusual ideas. Besides, the box itself may not be fully depleted. There may yet be a few good ideas rolling around that have not been implemented.

Out-of-the-box thinkers (and teachers) have to be careful and cautious. They may succeed if they have a plan of action that takes into account the social atmosphere for (or against) creativity. Or they may not. This pertains to many walks of life, from business to the classroom, from trade to politics, from personal relations to professional contacts (Sternberg et al. 2004).

Going outside the box may be fraught with problems. You may find yourself in another, perhaps larger, box filled with new problems, issues, and limitations. Worse yet, you may begin bouncing off the walls, allowing others to view you as a nonconformist or an eccentric.

Going outside of all the boxes is probably impossible. If we did so, the result might be so disorienting that we would not know what to make of it. Besides, at the end of the day, most of us are comfortable inside the box. We are much better at following tradition even when it is clearly failing. That is what most teachers do.

No changes, same old lesson plans. Wholly new territory is upsetting. Living within the box is always safest and least upsetting because of the human need for stability and predictability. Revolutions may be dangerous. Teaching, however, is not dangerous, even if the teacher changes dramatically. Most observers are not very good judges of teaching, creative or not, and may not even notice the changes.

Creativity, and creative teaching, implies change that may send you outside the box or off the walls. However, there is also a human need for excitement, adaptation, and adventure, which the box doesn't satisfy. We become bored with doing the same things over and over. Traditions seem stale and maladaptive. We are ready to grow.

We may even begin to want to change our instructional methods and our curricula.

So there we are as humans, as teachers, as students: caught between two basic needs, stability and adventure. We are told to think outside the box but fear what lies beyond.

CLASSROOMS IN THE BOX, OUTSIDE, OR BOUNCING OFF THE WALLS

In classrooms, as in business or politics, there is a great deal of talk about creativity, reform, efficiency, effectiveness, and invention, yet very little is realized. Labels change but content remains the same. The same content is poured into new electronic bottles.

Creativity in business is particularly valued and there are hundreds of books on innovation, change, new approaches, and yes, thinking outside the box (De Bono 1985, 1999). This is less true of education, at least at this point in time. Our emphasis on "reform" seems intent on merely reshaping the box. We hope for something new and improved, but seem bound by a tradition of "knowledge in, knowledge out."

Nevertheless, there is considerable opportunity for individual teachers or committed groups, or even schools or school systems as a whole, to promote creative teaching and learning. It begins with an analysis of the situation. What is the probability that this atmosphere favors innovation and change? Any system, whether local, state, or national, has a climate working for or against change and is subject to greater or lesser contradictory pressures from within and without that shape learning. At any given point in time, these may favor innovation, conformity, or something in between.

Clearly, the more open the environment as a whole, the more likely the production of creative ideas and lessons and programs. More repressive and hostile environments are less likely to foster the production of creative ideas, by either students or teachers. The same holds true for business and politics; freer settings usually produce more invention, and vice versa.

Classrooms are almost never as "open" as businesses to new ideas because teachers face more constraints. Many, if not all, programs and subjects are aimed at reproducing knowledge so students will be prepared for jobs, citizenship, and social relations.

Students must possess "needed" knowledge and skills that others have invented and refined long ago, though much of it may seem useless. Programs do not generally allow for a great deal of input from students or suggestions from parents. There is, to speak in a business metaphor, relatively little marketing or survey research in education, and almost nothing in the way of focus groups asking about customer satisfaction.

Thus, the box is fairly small and limited.

But the box can be opened to outside influence by tying the past to the present and the future. It can also be pried open a bit by linking codified knowledge to ongoing issues and problems. Careful connections beyond the classroom box can be parlayed into great excitement, making clear that the older knowledge has relevance and a relationship to the newer knowledge. Inventions don't come out of nowhere.

Students may begin to see beyond the box (particularly with a teacher's help) to the outside world they are being prepared to inhabit. They may then see the possibilities of breaching the box or leaping the walls.

They may even evince a modicum of interest.

MENTAL HEALTH: MADNESS AND EUPHORIA AFFECT CREATIVITY

For those playing teacher roles, whether parents, classroom teachers, leaders, or entrepreneurs, creativity is closely allied to mental health.

Contrary to the image of the mad genius, a hypertensive, creative, quixotic artist, social context has a lot to do with encouraging or inhibiting imagination. Renaissance men (and women!) are called that because the Renaissance in Europe altered the more settled and stricter medieval culture, promoting a wave of cultural and technological inventiveness. It was an age of experimentation, political ferment, and an expansion of popular culture.

But this level of creativity evolved over a long period of time and was quite unevenly distributed. To live in that age was probably most enjoyable and productive for teachers because they could espouse new ideas and practices with state or private support, and without serious repercussions. Setting, atmosphere, and tolerance really matter.

The same is true in schools. One might be driven by narrow learning goals, like success on tests, another by broader conversations about interpreting and applying knowledge. More exciting still is when knowledge is applied to present-day problems.

The school atmosphere yields, in turn, happier or sadder teachers, willing and able or unwilling and unable to develop exciting new curricular ideas. (Happiness or sadness may also be a reaction to "audiences"—students and administrations.)

Student audiences (of whatever age or origin) contribute significantly to a school's atmosphere. If the school has a high percentage of problems, difficult students who are apathetic and aggressive, then the overall atmosphere for creativity will likely be lessened or extinguished. The fires of imagination will smother under a dark haze of indifference, poor management, and antagonism. Those who are creative will go underground or leave.

In contrast, an interested student body that shows initiative in learning will draw out the best from creative teachers. Interesting lessons and formats will be developed and ideas and attitudes will be shared, forming a growing cycle of risk-taking and open-ended thinking. A new and richer creative atmosphere will evolve and take hold in the learning community (Sawyer 2007).

Thus, the context, the school, and the student body add up to a whole that promotes or inhibits opportunities for creative action. Teachers will emerge from their boxes to see what can be done, or burn out. How teachers feel—euphoric or "mad," excited or depressed—will affect all of their endeavors.

Euphoria, a sense of appreciation and empowerment, will develop from the positive social/school context, while a sense of "madness" or despair will grow out of a negative setting (Zevin 2010). Jumping out of the box takes support and encouragement from the other players in the game.

A teacher has to be energized to plan for creative lessons. Madness, a feeling of frustration, and lack of respect tend to diminish the push for invention and inventiveness. Euphoria, by contrast, is a feeling arising from audience (student) appreciation and participation and the vibrant exchanges of news and views. Support and encouragement from school leaders and administrators help a lot in creating a positive emotional state. Euphoria and madness are the polar opposites of emotion for teachers and the context for the rise or decline of creativity.

How, then, in our current context, can test scores improve or any sort of real learning occur when teachers are under pressure to perform within narrow conformist guidelines to achieve an unworthy objective: simple didactic data collection?

JUMPING OUT AND BEYOND THE GIVEN DATA
Climbing out of the box takes courage.

Teaching outside the standard curriculum requires imagination. To bounce, breach, surmount, and bounce off walls takes planning, skill, and deep knowledge. It also demands student support in the form of respect, appreciation, playfulness, and sharing ideas. Creative teaching outside the box and off the walls is basically social action: audience (students) and actress/actor (teacher) must work together. There is a union of interests and a tacit social contract between teachers and learners implying that they are going to have fun learning in unusual ways.

Teachers can integrate play with work so students begin to see work as play. A new structure for learning develops, one far more experimental than the usual literal and linear ways of thinking in a typical classroom. Teachers change position, move around, join student groups; students conduct hands-on research, draw their own conclusions, debate ideas with each other and with their teacher. Outcomes become far less predictable, and much more interesting.

The teacher's role morphs into a new dimension of partnership, although it still involves subtly guiding students toward a higher purpose. Students begin to understand that imagination and insight really count the most, more than simple knowledge, yet knowledge is not neglected. Ideas and questions tend to be initiated by students as the new social context evolves. In general, ideas take on more and more importance as the focus of teaching and learning, and they grow in power as the creative classroom develops.

The teacher gently evolves into a creative teacher, an exciting teacher.

CREATIVITY AND THE ELECTRONIC AGE

Age-old goals of teaching have included critical mindedness, Socratic inquiry, discovery learning, and constructivism, and all are within our grasp. Yet the geometrically increasing amount of data available electronically tends to overwhelm reasoning processes, smothering emotional and intellectual growth. We are suffering from information overload, lost in a "cloud"! We cannot separate the forest from the trees, the chaff from the wheat. We need guidance through the thickets of information and the computing "cloud." We need sharp wits to separate sales pitches from sound facts.

Surprisingly, thinking off the walls is theoretically enabled by the age of "free" information, yet our educational systems seem more and more obsessed with testing knowledge bases, more concerned about school organization and labels than content or method or (whoops!) philosophy.

Jumping outside the box calls for the will to experiment, combined with retrieval and application skills and judgment. These are higher-order mental operations that a creative teacher offers students in a rich and varied educational context, whether in a home, school, or business.

These are the skills and ideas that really matter, far more than encyclopedic compilations of "facts." After all, the "facts" can be located on the web and downloaded and (if your teacher doesn't get suspicious) turned in as "your" paper! To combat the Scylla and Charybdis of rote learning and information overload, a creative teacher needs strategies or "engines" that go well beyond the facts up into the higher levels of thought and action.

"ENGINES" FOR CREATIVE TEACHING

Finding strategies and methods that build student skills in engaging ways is a time-honored goal in the pedagogy of inquiry. However, creative teaching requires a variety of methods and a scaffold for assessing progress. In this area, the well-established taxonomies of instructional goals, first invented by Benjamin Bloom, can guide our planning. There are actually three taxonomies, the first for cognitive growth, the second for affective levels, and the third aimed at psychomotor skills (Anderson and Sosniak 1994).

The most popular cognitive taxonomy has been revised, placing "remembering," knowledge collection, at the lowest level and "creating," forming new meanings or structures, at the highest level of thinking. How nice! Receiving phenomena/attention is the lowest level of the affective domain, the highest being "internalizing values," the building of a value system. In the psychomotor domain, "perception," the use of sensory cues, is the lowest level, while the highest is "origination," creating new movements to solve specific problems.

The three taxonomies may be viewed as integrated and overlapping, shown below:

Affective (growth in feelings/emotions/attitudes)
Psychomotor (growth in physical skills)   **Cognitive** (growth in mental skills)

A set of strategies for teaching and learning will be derived from these three domains and applied throughout this book. The domains should be thought of as aimed at inventing and applying techniques that cut across all ages and disciplines. Furthermore, each domain should be conceived of as connected to and overlapping with the others.

Drawing connections between and among domains is a key to creative teaching, learning, and thinking (Gentner et al. 2001). Individuals can begin to view themselves in an instructional role as a "whole" teacher who meets a "whole" child.

Creating arises in settings where teachers, leaders, entrepreneurs, and customers are open to experimentation. The atmosphere must allow free discussion of ideas and promote sharing, drawing upon evidence-based insights from individuals and groups. This holistic view of pedagogy will allow us to work and play with instruction that engages both interested and reluctant learners.

Six "engines," or strategies, are suggested as tools for creative pedagogy. Each is designed to stimulate thinking, feeling, and action at increasingly higher levels.

These engines fuse cognition, affect, and psychomotor skills. They offer guidelines for developing and implementing curriculum and instruction that promote discovery and insight for students. Each engine reflects a level or stage of Bloom's taxonomy. However, stages may be considered and utilized as interlocking, overlapping sets, not distinct steps.

Teachers seeking creative approaches encourage movement up and down the ladder of stages. Movement depends on the progress and reaction of the students. Teachers are, after all, working to improve students, and they must begin with the recognizable before jumping out of the box.

The six engines of growth in teaching creatively are as follows:

Attention Awakened

Attention is awakened when teachers **ask about evidence and observation**: the close and careful scrutiny of the world around us, contact with raw materials, orientation to environments.

Questions about description and detail (remembering/receiving phenomena/ beginning perception—not memorizing!)

Ideas Aroused

Ideas are aroused when teachers **ask about meaning, message, and explanation**: understanding terms, developing categories, drawing analogies, and making metaphors.

Questions about definitions, concepts, and reasons (developing categories/ classifications/reasoning and hypothesizing)

Curiosity Sparked

Curiosity is sparked when teachers **ask about explanation and hypothesis**: applying and analyzing evidence, determining cause and effect, relationships and correlations, hypotheses and inferences.

Questions about reasons and hypotheses (application through analysis)

Investigations Stimulated
Investigations are stimulated when teachers **ask about perplexity and mystery**: multiple, clashing, and converging views, ambiguity and puzzlement, contradictions and unknowns.

Questions about possibilities and probabilities (analysis/organization/complex overt response)

Viewpoints Explored
Viewpoints are explored when teachers **ask about different perspectives and conflicting interpretations**: multiple, overlapping, converging, contradictory, and conflicting frames of reference.

Questions about vantage point and trustworthiness (synthesis/organization continued/adaptation)

Judgments Provoked (Stirred)
Judgments are provoked when teachers **ask about moral issues and material assessments**: criteria-based evaluations and moral values, controversies and commitments, debates and decisions, philosophical stands on good and evil.

Questions about judgments and ethical values (evaluating/internalizing values/origination)

CONCLUSION
A classroom or school setting conducive to creativity requires student support, cooperative leadership, community approval of goals, and a commitment to innovation. Of course, an open-minded teacher is a key player in this drama.

A Renaissance ethos engenders innovation and deep learning, giving teachers a sense of vibrancy and mental health that leads them to enrich the curriculum and attempt engaging pedagogies.

Thinking in the box is easy and safest. Thinking outside the box is riskier but with higher rewards, stimulating imagination. Thinking off the walls tests the limits of invention and imagination, sometimes leading to dead ends, sometimes to breakthroughs changing culture and society, maybe even schools and colleagues.

It is up to us, those playing the role of teacher in any walk of life—family, business, school, or job—to opt for production rather than just reproduction of knowledge. In the age of electronics, knowledge alone is easily obtainable, making thought more valuable. However, most teaching is still centered on delivering the already known and asking the usual questions.

Therefore, we can and should work toward insight and imagination, asking more than telling as we approach audiences. We proceed from lower and higher levels of thinking, affect, and psychomotor skills, remembering that the priority is to aim high.

Development is organic. Students need time for play as well as work. They require practice and periodic assessment, more than formal testing. And teachers need ways to measure progress as growth and performance, not simply acquisition.

Teachers and their avatars play the key roles in developing students and promoting real learning. Teachers need time to apply and experiment with new ideas and techniques, noting successes and failures. Creative teaching also demands an awareness of student potential, marking the baseline and noting growth and development into higher and higher realms of cognition, affect, and psychomotor skills.

This book provides suggestions, ideas, theories, and practical examples to help you make and model those choices in whatever educational setting you find yourself—school, home, profession, or business.

Escape the box and see what's outside, seek alternatives, test new strategies, open minds to new ideas and interpretations.

REFERENCES

Anderson, Lorin W., and Lauren A. Sosniak, eds. 1994. *Bloom's Taxonomy: A Forty-Year Retrospective.* Chicago: NSSE, University of Chicago Press, 1994.

De Bono, E. 1985, 1999. *Six Thinking Hats.* Boston: Little, Brown (reissued by MICA Management Resources).

Gentner, D., K. J. Holyoak, and B. N. Kokinov. 2001. *The Analogical Mind: Perspectives from Cognitive Science.* Boston: MIT Press.

Sawyer, R. K. 2007. *Group Genius: The Creative Power of Collaboration*. New York: Basic Books.

Sternberg, R., E. Grigorenko, and J. L. Singer. 2004. *Creativity*. Washington, DC: American Psychological Association.

Zevin, J. 2010. *Teaching on a Tightrope*. Lanham, MD: Rowman & Littlefield.

1

Creativity and Creative Teaching Defined

"The key question isn't 'What fosters creativity?' But it is why in God's name isn't everyone creative? Where was the human potential lost? How was it crippled? I think therefore a good question might be not why do people create? But why do people not create or innovate? We have got to abandon that sense of amazement in the face of creativity, as if it were a miracle if anybody created anything."

—Abraham Maslow

"Creativity is inventing, experimenting, growing, taking risks, breaking rules, making mistakes, and having fun."

—Mary Lou Cook

WHAT'S THE BIG DEAL WITH CREATIVITY?

People often talk about creativity in reverential tones, but most of us don't have a very clear idea of what we mean when we use this word. Our society says it places great value on creativity, entrepreneurship, individuality, imagination, and inventiveness, particularly in business and the arts. We celebrate a select few successes in each area, treating these people as icons of achievement. We look up to and celebrate those who have made innovations

FIGURE 1.1

in sports, medicine, business, and the arts, particularly those who have made money, a lot of money.

Yet money and creativity are not necessarily closely related. In fact, the opposite may be true. People who achieve a degree of financial success may opt for the "tried and true" over the innovative and daring. Witness the number of business and political leaders and artists whose careers "stall out" because they cease to take chances.

Creativity is natural to humans and begins with play. For children, play is a path to discovery of the world around them. It usually involves deep observation (in their terms) and a fascination with something they discover about plants, animals, space, planets, or people. At first, play is relatively unstructured. Structure is imposed later by parents, and schools, and managers, which probably doesn't help creativity very much! Purpose emerges as children mature. Schools tend to build more and more structure into learning as children progress and play mutates into "work."

As work gains ground, imagination tends to be shunted aside, suppressed or overlooked. Work is often totally regimented, forming one half of a dichotomy: play vs. work, structure vs. freedom. Ironically, many businesses today strive to revive creativity using tools such as staff retreats, "icebreaking" activities during meetings and training sessions, and other forms of endorsed and encouraged play. Where did we lose that impulse to play and experiment? Sadly, it disappears in school and at work.

WHAT IS CREATIVITY?

Creativity is a term commonly used for actions that involve imagination, inventiveness, "business" acumen, and the making of unusual choices. Creative behavior extends and reconfigures the ordinary, the usual, and the traditional. "New" ideas are considered creative, as are new products, arguments, and theories, although most of them develop in a perfectly understandable evolutionary line. Growth and creativity represent a "peak experience" and a healthy sense of self-confidence (Maslow 1999, 183–97).

Creativity is linking or "reconfiguring" ideas that have not been integrated before, putting evidence into a general explanation that we might call a new theory or interpretation. Much of what is labeled creative connects previously unconnected ideas and findings into a more coherent whole. It may also involve an extension or extrapolation of an existing idea to new situations or products.

Defining creativity is a popular sport, but there is general agreement on a few major components. Boden suggests three:

1. reconnection: making unfamiliar combinations of familiar ideas,
2. exploration: expanding the conceptual space for investigation within an existing structure, and
3. transformation: changing/reconfiguring the landscape for thinking (Boden 2004, 2–3).

As a real-life example, Apple Computers linked design with several new innovations in programming and screen technology to come up with a more intuitive telephone, the iPhone. While the combination is new, the product itself might be described as a cross between a computer and a traditional phone with Internet service. Brisk sales led to Apple cofounder and CEO Steve Jobs being described as a "creative genius," although what he and a large staff of advisors, designers, and technicians really managed to do was combine existing parts and technology into a new whole with a sense of style.

Creativity is an ability to *extend, connect, and invent* new products, ideas, and interpretations that bring together disparate facts and factors into a more cohesive whole. However, this is not as easy as it looks. A supportive social atmosphere or open environment is necessary to foster new ideas and encourage experimentation. This holds true for business, labor, the arts, education, and society as a whole.

What will we achieve if we apply this creative paradigm to our current fact-laden and skills-heavy curricula? A great deal for the students.

MENTAL HEALTH

Creativity is a deeply embedded human disposition to explore that extends and enlivens us. In effect, creativity is a path to discovery of the world, its citizens, and one's own being. Learning is deepened through close observation and questioning, going where one has not gone before. New insights, feelings, and understandings are gathered and reflected upon, perhaps leading to a big idea or two, and greater satisfaction with life. There is a sense of "joy" in learning!

Creativity, therefore, is part of mental health, opening up opportunity, giving way to experimentation and the development of new interests and skills.

Creativity is about experimentation, going outside the "box," moving on to newer and more mind-expanding materials. We are not abandoning tradition, just experimenting with innovation and new choices. Remember, almost all creativity grows out of what went before by extension, connection, reconfiguration, and invention.

GROWTH

Creativity is vital for intellectual and physical growth. We feel healthier when we exercise our bodies *and our minds*. We need variety and the chance to jump out of the box.

Rote learning pounded into our brains is efficient, perhaps, in building knowledge, but it is not very effective in building thoughtfulness or skills. Memory is weak without emotional attachments, and it doesn't do much for a sense of accomplishment.

We need stimulation from within and without to grow, particularly from new ways of looking at the world and our place in it. A major step toward creativity is keeping our minds open to new ideas, techniques, activities, and interests. Then we play with our discoveries to find out what we really enjoy. We may pursue certain careers because of experiences in school and seek adventures that expand our intellects. If we build emotional attachment, it makes us feel we are getting smarter and more capable, livelier. These are signs of intellectual and physical growth. For example, we may try out a sport or an exercise we had never heard of and really find it exhilarating. Zumba! All of a sudden we begin to dance. Or we may begin to read theoretical books by heavyweights on a subject we've always been interested in. All of a sudden, we have something to say about politics. We start writing letters to the editor! We follow the news more avidly.

We may read a book about bird life and sit in the park noticing little warblers for the first time. Or we may take an art or music class and find out we are talented! Then we start listening to new recordings, discovering music we never dreamed of that satisfies and enriches. We may take up art beginning with painting by numbers. But we sign up for several art classes and find out we have real style. Then we dump paint by numbers and structure in favor of developing our own techniques.

Expanding horizons and openness to new experiences give us a feeling we are growing and entering a new social network. We are building self-confidence in new areas of interest.

SOCIAL NETWORKING

Creativity offers the potential for group action as well as individual initiative. Contrary to popular opinion, the solitary genius locked in a lab or studio probably never really existed. Most of our inventions and creations have been heavily influenced by our surroundings. Icons like Mozart, Einstein, Edison, or Gandhi, for example, were all influenced by community traditions, colleagues, fathers and mothers, teachers, and leaders, not to mention the society at large.

Many people they influenced were also influences upon them. Creative endeavors are a two-way street. Creativity therefore is not a thing in and of itself. It is a product of a complex set of social interactions, in contemporary parlance, a social network.

EXPLORATION

Creativity is all about relatively *open exploration*. You are left alone to muse, ponder, mull things over, and make a leap, not directed to a particular conclusion or template. There is also perhaps a touch of obsession required. Discovery, even of something already discovered by others, is a very healthy experience because learners must work the problem through by studying the evidence. It is an avatar of the original.

Exploration is a great way to teach observational skills, and close observation is a basic process in creativity. If you cannot or don't recognize the details of your studies, whether art, science, social studies, or sports, it is unlikely that deep knowledge will result.

If you are a skilled scout and can find your way out of the forest by compass, stars, landscape, and landmarks, that is a lot more impressive than following a marked trail with a beginning and end set by the rangers. They've done most of the work, not you.

Some fine discoveries have taken place in the most humble surroundings, such as Piaget's theory of child development, which arose from him sitting in the schoolyard watching kids play marbles. Einstein's Theory of Relativity was born in a study long before our sophisticated space telescopes and cyclotrons were invented.

The point is that exploration is about noticing what others step over or around, trying to make sense of it. Exploration and observation are closely linked. And through these two discovery is engendered. Explanation grows out of discovery and then more important ideas evolve, but these grow in a social context. And time is allowed or taken to use all the senses in a hands-on, tactile, visual, and auditory experience and experiment.

CREATIVITY AND LEARNING

Context can encourage or inhibit ideas. A culture that values entrepreneurship, for example, makes rules and permits investments to encourage the risk-taker, the promoter of new ideas and products. Conversely, a closed and authoritarian society, where freedom of speech is suppressed and new ideas are suspect, is unlikely to create a large class of inventors. And so it is with learning. A tightly ordered classroom looks good in the sense that there is a place for everything and everything is in its place (including the students), but that order may yield only reproduction and build memory banks, not ideas.

Critics often berate schools for lacking imagination. They argue that schools do not foster new ideas or produce the leaders that we need. But just a few breaths later, the same critics claim schools do not adequately prepare students in basics like mathematics and reading. This schizophrenic view of the role of schools has increased dramatically in recent years, to the detriment of the creativity the schools are supposed to encourage.

While creativity is linked to a sense of the "free spirit," open to new experiences and ideas, school success is linked to a rather intense and directed regimen of knowledge acquisition needed for good test scores. These are the contradictory goals of schools and school systems meant to combine higher-order thinking, that is, reaching the borderline of creativity while at the same time stuffing students full of huge quantities of information that are rarely put to real use. We want productivity and skills, but increasingly seek to achieve them by demanding narrower and narrower forms of behavior and curriculum. We want instant results, rather than waiting for the more organic growth natural to humans. Play is cut short and work takes precedence.

In contrast, students who recognize that they have advanced into and mastered new territory are usually quite pleased with themselves and most likely pleased with their teacher. How is this different from a "typical" classroom? Consider spending the rest of your life eating at the same restaurant, driving the same car, going on exactly the same vacation, or reading the same authors. After a while, life becomes a series of repetitive behaviors and repetitive thoughts. Far from joy, you probably feel apathetic. Taking notes off a blackboard, SMARTboard, or screen or copying the "correct" answers to questions from a textbook account produce a similar effect. A true learning experience, in contrast, expands skills and improves confidence.

In addition, the social and collaborative potential of creativity can be a great boon. It can help students adjust to and connect with their peers. Listening to others promotes cross-checking and corroboration, with the proviso that there is a solid base of observation and data. Students will also learn that many minds are better than one, as our earlier Apple example clearly showed.

Creativity does not take place in a vacuum or by a lone genius cut off from everyone.

It could even happen in schools and at work.

WHAT DOES IT MEAN TO TEACH CREATIVELY?

If there is much to be gained, for students and society, from creativity, then teachers must be able to foster and nurture this innate ability. Teaching creatively requires the teacher to play unusual roles. Creative work includes higher-order thinking, hands-on invention, and insightful breakthroughs that are new to learners. (It is conceivable that the ideas are new to everyone, but this is rare, and greatly to be treasured.)

Teachers who seek to promote and encourage creative learning plan to stimulate thinking, insight, and invention using a variety of methods. These methods have been variously termed inquiry, discovery, critical thinking, and constructivism. While terms and conceptions differ, creative methods share a deep commitment to student involvement with evidence and higher-order thinking. Students learn to observe, interpret, and synthesize *without* benefit of text or teacher leading them directly to the "correct" answers. In creative classrooms, answers are negotiable and outcomes often uncertain or ambiguous.

A teacher working toward a creative classroom builds questioning levels and presents provocative data. The whole point of a creative approach is to stimulate thinking and feeling and psychomotor skills, promoting a search for evidence in which students participate directly. Students are in effect creating interpretations and hypotheses that explain problems at hand. They are also developing inquiry and critical thinking skills along the way.

Creative teaching does NOT imply that the students *will* or *must* become creative. The teacher's goal is developing those habits of mind that will lead to creative thinking. Achieving this takes a great deal of skill. Reaching uniformly high levels of creative insight (creativity in the wider sense) is a whole other matter, a very ambitious goal achieved only once in a while. Actual invention of new ideas, products, and connections is even more unusual, particularly in an educational setting. A creative classroom need not produce patents and copyrights, only increase thinking levels for greater understanding and emotional growth. A creative classroom builds a platform for creativity and a scaffold for advancement.

WHO IS A CREATIVE TEACHER?

A creative teacher is someone like you and me who decides that he or she wants to stimulate student ideas, build interest, and promote participation. These teachers resist teaching their subject as a "grocery list" (Van Sledright 2002) or a telephone book. Such a decision entails a push toward higher-order thinking, most especially the insight and imagination associated with intellectual breakthroughs. Usually, a creative teacher conducts a classroom that is interactive and involving, hands-on and dynamic.

This teacher is devoted to widening participation through individual and group work that fosters communication between and among students. Teachers trying to instruct creatively tend to set problems and act as guides rather than dominate an inquiry (Sternberg and Williams 1996). They usually avoid direct instruction or forcing specific answers ("fishing around" for the exact words they wish to hear).

Creative teachers perceive play as a natural part of the classroom environment, as we'll see in the following chapter. And they view their students as capable of making great strides at their own pace across several dimensions—cognitive, affective, and psychomotor (Craft, Jeffrey, and Liebling 2001). Learners are provided with a classroom environment that promotes investigation and exploration, and time for reflection.

Skills are developed within the context of learning. In other words, the creative teacher becomes a partner rather than a boss and constructs a new environment for discovery, an environment that challenges students' views of the subject at hand, as well as of themselves and how they learn (Gardner 1993).

Creativity takes courage and a well-thought-out plan of action, but has many benefits.

CONCLUSION

In the broadest sense, creativity is the product of many cooperative, competing, and conflicting forces. Political atmosphere, economics, education, and society all play key roles in supporting or inhibiting creative impulses. Social atmosphere affects schools, work, home, and all organizations (Ray 1990).

The more conformity is demanded (in a classroom or society at large), the greater the reproduction of existing ideas. Less attention is paid to extending thinking, connecting to the unusual, or the invention of something really innovative. Social milieu is therefore vitally important to the overall level of creation and production (Csikszentmihalyi 1988).

Schools play a modest role in this process, mostly because teachers see their mission as didactic and informative rather than reflective and imaginative. Think of our common metaphors for instruction: drum in knowledge, toe the line, cover ground, and remember facts. All betray the essentially reproductive nature of schooling. Herein lies the rub. Facts are needed for thinking, indeed, but the thinking must go beyond the facts. Facts are the building blocks, not the edifice. Powerful questions hold the keys to creative thinking in all settings (Leeds 2000).

Facts alone are not enough for intellectual, physical, or emotional breakthroughs to new, higher levels. We need (as a society and as individuals) an atmosphere in which the explorer, inventor, or thinker is encouraged to grow, to experiment, and eventually create. We need a feeling of health, the warmth of encouragement, and a sense of self-worth. Others around you are doing the same and approve of your endeavors.

Creative teachers provide facts, but as data open to interpretation, drawing students into problems that stimulate insights about any given subject. Students must be active in the process of teaching, and the teacher must recognize and reward that partnership (Khatena 1978).

A lively class contributes to a playful atmosphere for creative thinking, encouraging the creative teacher to reciprocate. The atmosphere is lively, but open to making mistakes. The creative teacher must be a partner in learning, both giving and gaining approval and appreciation from the class.

Reciprocity, partnership, challenge, and a sense of bewilderment help us all to leap out of the box and seek alternative paths to discovery and invention.

Once out of the box we can bounce off the walls of new ideas.

REFERENCES

Boden, M. A. 2004. *The Creative Mind: Myths and Mechanisms*. New York: Routledge.

Craft, A., B. Jeffrey, and M. Liebling, eds. 2001. *Creativity in Education*. New York: Continuum Press.

Csikszentmihalyi, M. 1988. "Society, Culture, and Person: A Systems View of Creativity." In *The Nature of Creativity*, edited by R. J. Sternberg. New York: Cambridge University Press.

Gardner, H. 1993. *Creating Minds.* New York: Basic Books.

Khatena, J. 1978. *The Creatively Gifted Child: Suggestions for Parents and Teachers.* New York: Vantage Press.

Leeds, Dorothy. *The Seven Powers of Questions: Secrets to Successful Communication in Life and Work.* New York: Berkley Publishing Group, 2000.

Maslow, A. H. 1968, 1999, 3rd ed. *Toward a Psychology of Being.* New York: John Wiley and Sons.

Ray, Michael. 1990. *Creativity in Organizations.* Stanford, CA: Stanford University Press.

Sternberg, R. J., and W. M. Williams. 1996. *How to Develop Student Creativity.* Alexandria, VA: Association for Supervision and Curriculum Development.

Van Sledright, B. 2002. *In Search of America's Past.* New York: Teacher's College/ Columbia University.

Work and Play, Play and Work

The Genesis of Creativity

"'I don't think they play at all fairly,' Alice began, in rather a complaining tone, 'and they all quarrel so dreadfully one can't hear oneself speak— and they don't seem to have any rules in particular: at least, if there are, nobody attends to them—and you've no idea how confusing it is all the things being alive: for instance, there's an arch I've got to go through next walking about at the other end of the ground—and I should have croqueted the Queen's hedgehog just now, only it ran away when it saw mine coming!' 'How do you like the Queen?' said the Cat in a low voice. 'Not at all,' said Alice: 'she's so extremely—.'"

—Lewis Carroll, *The Annotated Alice*, 113–14

INTRODUCTION: CURIOSITY

Curiosity is a powerful human motivation.

Children and young adults have a wonderful natural sense of curiosity that often drives their play. This is quite healthy because a great deal of research indicates that play is an important source of practice for children and youth (Bruner, Jolly, and Sylvia 1976). In effect, young people are experimenting with new skills and ideas, as well as learning important social/emotional behaviors. A voyage of discovery is taking place, unfettered by imposed goals.

Play is the beginning and foundation of literacy and numeracy through creative behavior (Bruner 1983).

The idea of play as healthy and natural, providing children with a form of
training for life, is not particularly new. But it is not always taken seriously
past preschool and the early grades. Schools frequently see themselves as
places where children and young adults learn to work, follow schedules, and
meet deadlines.

While this may be acceptable training for adult life and preparation for
work, the emphasis on work sometimes destroys the sense of play. As a result,
we suffer a loss in two areas: higher-level/creative thinking and the development of social skills. However, work and play are not mutually exclusive.

In fact, play and work may be viewed as operating in and out of learning
across several dimensions: psychomotor, cognitive, and affective (Anderson
et al. 2001). These dimensions are interlocking parts in the overall scheme of
creative teaching and learning, as the chart below shows.

Affective domain

Psychomotor domain   **Cognitive domain**

FIGURE 2.1

BRIDGING THE GAP BETWEEN WORK AND PLAY

Work has been defined as accomplishing an objective for some type of reward: personal, practical, or monetary (Sylva et al. 1976). Usually, work is highly structured, with specified steps that must be completed to achieve the desired end.

Consider cooking as an example. Cooking can be work or play. When you follow a recipe so your family can have dinner on time and get on to more important tasks, cooking isn't play. If you innovate and create your own recipe, experiment with new ingredients, or want to show off your elegant skills, then this type of work begins to take on aspects of play. Cuisine becomes artistic and ego-involving, "show-personship" as you invent. Dining becomes entertainment.

Unfortunately, education often follows a recipe. Much of a teacher's life is spent directing traffic. Control is critical. Direction is vital. Authority is asserted. But, alas, authority, direction, and control, even if done well, do very little to promote interest, understanding, or creativity. It is a recipe we have inherited, sometimes for good reasons, but it is not our own creation.

Consider an elementary school where children of many backgrounds and abilities are in the same classrooms. They vary greatly in knowledge and comfort with school. To extend the analogy, it's a very disparate mix of ingredients that probably won't lend itself easily to a traditional recipe. A new and innovative approach—a new recipe—is needed.

PLAY AND PLAYFULNESS

Play is an activity that has its own rules and the outcomes are usually open (Gilmore 1985). A child or young adult plays voluntarily and has the right to

FIGURE 2.2
Blind men and elephant. From *Golden Treasury Readers: Primer*, by C. M. Stebbins and M. H. Coolidge (New York: American Book Co., 1909), 48.

opt in or out, as he or she wishes. Play is much freer than work because outcomes are not so clear and the desired product is unspecified.

Play is a form of self-expression that, if satisfying, produces intense concentration and involvement, and some degree of emotion. For instance, emotions arise when someone wins or loses a game, or when a friend and ally turns away from you to another for support and friendship. Much depends upon your attitude toward play and how much you want a specific outcome. You are demonstrating skills to yourself and to others. And you are a volunteer.

As pressures for success increase, play becomes more and more like work. Judgment is involved and you lose intrinsic interest and self-motivation. For example, ballet or Little League can be a lot of fun as "play" activities. Yet if your dance teacher or coach is strongly accomplishment-oriented and insists on doing the job—winning—according to a very particular set of rules, you are at work.

Play is usually unfettered in the sense that the child or adult pursues what pleases or interests them. Play and playfulness usually involve choice and self-direction combined with relatively uncertain objectives (Fredrickson 2001). This is not true of work. In play, children or adults can win, lose, or even quit. There may be social pressures, but what to do is still their decision.

What propels them to play is fascination with their own bodies (as in sports), with their feelings (as in socializing), and with their minds (as in puzzles or mysteries). Children can be easily drawn into problems or mysteries, like the nature and composition of rocks, reasons for shifting weather patterns, or what causes a sudden outburst of emotion. It's like being a detective examining clues to solve a puzzle. Young adults and adults may be similarly motivated.

By its very nature, creativity is personal and satisfying, although the product may not be very original or useful. The point is that play is "original" *for the student.* It is the feeling of discovery that counts. Playful "experimentation" can suddenly produce powerful and surprising insights. This is often less true of work because its goals are far more purposeful.

The positive side of work is that it provides all of us, children and youth included, with a sense of accomplishment measured against (hopefully clear) standards or goals. We all feel proud of ourselves. Pat yourself on the back for reading twenty biographies and bask in the glow of kind words from your teacher. Won the spelling bee: cool!

Work also gets a bad rap on occasion, particularly when the pressures are great or the task is so controlled or rushed that it seems like torture. Doing the same thing over and over again can really get boring! Repetitive tasks have been shown to diminish positive attitudes and kill interest (Duffy 1998). No room is left for personal development or exploration. Stress takes its toll in these situations.

Work can offer us mastery of a body of knowledge or technique, like driving, but only infrequently encourages innovations or problem solving. After all, in work the problem has already been set and the solution is pretty clear. In play, there is the challenge of identifying the problem and then finding a strategy for a solution.

PLAY AS WORK; WORK AS PLAY

Work and play are usually portrayed as quite different behaviors. Work is structured, directed by others, and goal-oriented; play is unstructured, self-directed, and perhaps goalless. Yet close analysis yields similarities (Singer and Singer 1977). Play can be goal-directed, particularly formal games or simulations. Play-acting, for example, may be directed toward a goal of imitation, fantasy, or, for older students, satire. This requires work to be imaginative! Thus play and work share some aims and features.

Why do children (or adults, for that matter) play? Theories have explained play as behavior that springs from psychological and social roots. These theories, especially those of Piaget and Ellis, stress play as a means of developing intellect and creativity by seeking excitement.

Children and youth come to grips with problems presented by the outside world that are difficult to understand at first. Play, in this view, is a way of adapting to new and unfamiliar demands by experimenting with ideas and acting out fantasies. Children and young people are working to impose their own way of thinking on the complex problems and issues of daily life (Fein 1986), a process that changes with maturity.

As children grow and develop, their ability to manipulate the world increases. Play is a way of testing their newly developed competence by solving self-imposed problems or by participating in games that allow competition and cooperation. The overriding goal of play is practice inventing, finding, and solving problems.

Games are part of discovering both the self and the outside world. Whether physical, electronic, or social, games allow the player mastery and fantasy.

Games themselves offer greater or lesser opportunities depending on the kind and degree of inference and skill demanded. A very tightly structured electronic game, for example, offers a good deal less playfulness than a more open game that invites role development and wider choice, and vice versa.

From a psychological and intellectual standpoint, play can be viewed as a search for physical, social, and mental stimulation. Children do not direct their energy everywhere, but usually channel their powers into physical and intellectual challenges. They may draw, build with blocks, play on a computer, ride a scooter, or play a team sport such as basketball. Or they may just wander around picking things up and examining them or taking them apart. As we get older, these activities are often termed "hobbies."

All of these interests and entertainments reflect goals, although the outcomes may not be immediately productive or useful. All have some sort of structure that is like work, but not as clear-cut or well defined. In fact, the whole point of play, according to theorists, is that it is *not* as directed and well-structured as work (King 1982a).

If play is a child's way of testing her- or himself, of pushing toward greater competence and understanding, it is more appealing if problems are open and poorly structured. If problems are wholly solved, then how can competence be tested or discoveries made about the world? Handling interesting and thought-provoking materials and making a mess is fun. Creativity is generally enjoyable and self-propelled, not imposed or directed. If we define play as a search for stimulating ideas and physical challenges, then play is continuous with, rather than distinct from, work.

Play is also part of many segments of the curriculum, especially those in which we hope to encourage reasoning, imaginative thinking, problem-solving, and self-expression (Furth and Wachs 1974). A creative teacher takes advantage of natural curiosity and the drive for competence to challenge students. Play can be harnessed to promote work. Work and play can fuse to enhance understanding and thinking.

Harnessing Play in a Classroom

A major way to harness play in the interest of serious learning is through puzzles, games, or game-like materials and lessons. Games build on playfulness by challenging students to win some prize or reach a solution that demonstrates their skill and determination. Psychomotor skills, feelings, and knowledge all come into play (Bruner 1983).

Games may involve team or individual effort and rewards may be intrinsic (the satisfaction of winning) or extrinsic (five extra points on your next grade). Teachers are often far more interested in the learning outcomes than in the winning, which may be a false value. The format and style of a game may be used to promote both educational and creative goals.

The most effective puzzles and games are generally open-ended with variable outcomes. There are many roadblocks and problems, chance factors, and difficult decisions along the way. Problems that challenge are what people enjoy when they play a game. Some of the classic board games are still popular because they are open to different strategies, such as Clue, Monopoly, and chess. To the extent that an outcome is known in advance, a game becomes more like work, and also a good deal less interesting.

Whodunits or mysteries, for example, are fun challenges. It may be frustrating and annoying to be diverted by false clues, unreliable witnesses, and mistakes of interpretation, but you stick with it anyway because you want a solution. The process may be as enjoyable as the solution, that is, detecting motives, picking up clues, and making deductions. You become a junior Sherlock Holmes, working hard but thinking it is play.

Teaching creatively involves converting ordinary material or topics into these types of games or game-like structures (King 1982b). Even rather uninteresting and didactic topics can be redesigned. A sense of "playing the game" encourages pursuit and the development of problem-solving skills in any subject.

Play and Problem Solving

Play and work are close allies in a classroom. The key is building a lesson around a problem that students feel *must* be solved. Problems come in many sizes, shapes, and colors, the simplest of which involves the processing of raw data and primary sources.

These may be cartoons, songs, charts and graphs, reading materials, films, reports, maps, newspaper columns, numbers, experiments, textbooks, paintings, and stories, or dates, names, and places. Whatever is used, students need time to work with the materials in a nonjudgmental atmosphere. They need free, unfettered time to search and reflect, without any specific product in mind.

As students get used to creative learning, more complex problems may be designed to foster rigorous thinking at higher levels. Problems should be increasingly challenging—"wicked" types that are open-ended or difficult to solve (Conklin 2006). Students play with reasoning and use logic, symbols, and syllogisms. Playing with reasoning involves looking at ways we develop conclusions using our data to learn how to learn. Players also learn to work with each other cooperatively, or in mild conflict, both opening creative possibilities (Kreidler 1984).

Teachers can easily encourage play with reasoning in almost any context with phrases such as "jumping to conclusions," "stereotyping," or "bandwagon." Thinking out loud becomes part of play (and work). Examples may be offered of people drawing conclusions too quickly without really checking their facts. Prejudicial remarks can be identified and criticized using questions about the truth or falsehood of generalizations (stereotypes): words such as "all' or "none," "them" or "us," as in "all Europeans are blue-eyed blonds," or "they are not like us."

There are many opportunities to play with the bandwagon idea, the notion of "doing something because everyone else is doing it," conforming to what is trendy. For example, is it reasonable to say that you should buy the "blow them away" video game just because it is popular? Playing with reasoning grows naturally out of almost any lesson because we draw conclusions using too little data and make false assumptions.

Inconsistencies and contradictions abound and are fun to point out (especially if they are not yours). Syllogisms are easily punctured once you get the hang of it (as long as you demolish them in a friendly manner). After all, despite the fact that all fish swim in the water, when Alex swims in the water he doesn't actually qualify as a fish. Insights about knowledge and feelings grow in this kind of atmosphere and are indicative of a new comfort level with thinking out loud.

Gadzooks! Now we have the beginnings of creativity!

The process may be more difficult than creating the problem: playing with values involves an examination and a judgment of the beliefs that people hold and act on. Values are composed of at least two dimensions: evidence-based judgments (conventional, rational) and moral judgments (emotional, philosophical).

Deciding which computer is a best buy is evidence-based, while deciding if there is such a thing as a just war is ethical and emotional. Value claims grow out of different points of view or judgments about quality that require some

---

OFF THE WALLS THINKING

Let's create and design our own classroom money. Let's build a school out of LEGOs. Let's paint our own hands as puppets. Let's decide the color of dinosaurs from our own research. Let's find out which shapes are "strongest": circles, squares, or triangles. Let's make a list of the best jokes ever and create a rating scale. Let's do a play laughing and crying at all the wrong times and find out how we feel about it.

---

knowledge of the facts. Defending a value position builds on other levels of play, incorporating data and reasons, feelings and attitudes, while moving toward a real choice or position.

There are many play-like avenues for taking positions and making judgments. These include mock trials, debates, and role-playing. Students can take the place of someone with values different from their own. Be forewarned, feelings can run deep and may cause outbursts of passion, welcome and unwelcome.

Students usually see this type of play as taking part in a drama that mimics real life, but maintains a comfortable distance from taking action. In playing with values and feelings, there is always time to consider another's ideas and emotions, and to reconsider, delay, or strengthen attitudes and decisions. Creative teachers seek this kind of fluidity to enhance toleration and encourage consideration of alternative views.

It is perfectly acceptable in play to give up, to experiment, to fantasize about possibilities, to challenge, to dawdle once in a while, and to admit to being stuck. Social play gives learners the chance to compare and contrast conclusions, feelings, and choices. It is also a way of taking a measure of views they may like or shy away from. In play, examining data, comparing alternatives, and pondering choices aloud is acceptable. At work, you are pushed to a conclusion, behavior, skill, or product, often with an authority watching.

Playing with ideas and values may continue over a long period of time. A final conclusion is not really desirable from a pedagogical point of view because this closes off alternatives. If a learner becomes tired of a problem in midstream, he or she can move on to a new topic or issue, or interrupt it with other work and then return to the problem. Play and work should intertwine in mutual support of learning, each offering different strategies, providing a rest from routines or overheated competitions.

Creative teaching, therefore, mines the value of play-as-learning to choose and defend viewpoints and values.

SETTING UP WORK/PLAY, PLAY/WORK ENVIRONMENTS

The General Environment

The classroom environment you create is vitally important for promoting learning and socializing. For example, the way seating is arranged can inhibit or encourage interaction. Materials are displayed to invite or depress interest. The quantity and quality of equipment and books available can evoke or deaden curiosity.

Research has provided us with some general guidelines for building an inviting classroom, both in physical and psychological terms (King 1982a). Even in a rather old and dismal building, a great deal can be accomplished to alleviate the sense of being in an institution. In a modern building, it is relatively easy to arrange seating, materials, and activities to foster inquiry and discovery. So there are no excuses for rigid rows! Whatever the setting, a great deal can be done, often at low cost, to provide a sense of openness and an invitation to explore.

Theoretically, electronics can enhance communication in groups, but often everyone is simply watching a screen up at the front of a room. Media can be arranged to facilitate discussion or research if arranged informally as work stations.

A Rich Variety of Materials

In a creative classroom, there should be a rich variety of materials available that appeal to the senses: touching, handling, feeling, looking, listening, and thinking. They should appeal to all the senses, including the sixth. Materials stimulate thinking and participation in problem-solving.

In the elementary grades, one corner of the room could hold a dozen or so of the very best picture or storybooks, with questions inserted in each for students to answer as they read. Another corner might have a display of "critters" for scientific observation. A third corner could house a display of shapes ranging from squares to dodecahedrons, and a fourth corner a display of students' art based on their first encounter with an artist of choice.

An inexpensive CD player and a few dozen CDs of unusual and unfamiliar folk music should be on a shelf. A microphone should be attached so students can compose their own songs. Art folders with puzzling paintings and photographs that provoke imagination and promote interpretation should also have a space. A box of photographs may come with instructions and questions.

At least two or three dedicated computers should be loaded with several mysterious games, with a sign-up sheet for researchers or players. There might be a suggestion screen for activities using the computer, including entries by students who tell other students which games and websites really impressed them. Old and new textbooks should be stacked on a table to invite comparison. And, of course, there ought to be a couple of dictionaries and a thesaurus for serious writers.

Finally every office, schoolroom, waiting area, and station in the nation needs a varied pile of magazines to inspire new ideas. These should include

---

TEXTBOX 2.2

INSIDE THE BOX

What would you keep in your room to encourage young people to pay attention to history, literature, mathematics, or other areas of study? Which books, magazines, things, artifacts, or equipment would you consider *most* essential to stimulate the formation of ideas?

current issues and old journals with pictures that can be cut out. The room
will be a bit crowded and messy perhaps, but the environment will be rich in
suggestion and imagination.

Arranging the Furniture

Arrange chairs and tables to encourage interaction and cooperation. Flexible seating is preferable to fixed seating, allowing you to group and regroup
chairs and tables for different purposes. Cooperative learning might be organized into little circles while "show and tell" sessions could be enhanced
using a big circle.

Tables could be set up in small or large rectangles or squares to facilitate
hands-on projects involving cutting, pasting, and building activities. A small
puppet theater or a dramatic acting corner could be used for shows and dramatic readings. Secondary students might perform more sophisticated readings
and plays. Costumes could be researched and created if the means are available.

Ceilings and windowsills should not be overlooked. They can be festooned
with hanging mobiles, puzzles, maps, posters, or charts distributed around
the entire room and, if permitted, the ceiling as well!

And, of course, in addition to our classroom computers, it would be nice to
have a SMARTboard and a dozen or so iPads around the room. But beware.
These may be distracting as well as enriching. This depends on programming,
direction, and the ever-watchful surveillance of the creative teacher. Engagement with problems and classmates is the key to using interactive technologies (Dede 2009).

Remember that we are arranging a room with equipment and materials to
foster the creative potential of teachers and students.

There should be a variety of furniture in the room. The teacher's desk or
central place ought to be near the side center of the room where you can easily
survey the whole class in action, either as a large group, subdivided into small
units, or as individuals.

The seating should be changed to suit the activities. Some might be suited
to circles or semicircles like the Assembly of ancient Athens. Round or little
square tables for four can be lovely. Set up tables for small groups working on
projects. Soviet-style lines of desks facing forward would better fit a lecture, or
an army. Quaker meetings with groups facing an open square would facilitate
discussion, while two lines of face-to-face seats could mimic the debate struc-

---

TEXTBOX 2.3

INSIDE THE BOX

Room Plans A, B, C, D, and E (straight rows, circles, squares, two sides, round tables): Which do you think are most conducive to work and play? Which setting do you think will produce 50% or less talk time for teacher, 50% or more for students, 25% between and among students? Try it out!

■

---

ture of the British parliament. Keep track of which arrangements facilitate the most discussion and greatest exchange of views between teacher and students and among students.

USING TIME CREATIVELY

Time is also part of an environment, work, home, or school. Time is important because it is a scarce and valuable resource that is often overlooked in designing a rich and varied classroom. However, in educational endeavors, time often creates unnecessary problems. For example, the pressure to "cover" a body of facts is often interpreted by teachers as meaning that they must rush through materials at top speed. Students must be ready for a test, quiz, survey, state, city, national examination, and so on.

Despite pressures, most curricular materials allow for a degree of reflection, judgment, and interpretation. There is an opportunity here to choose: quality or quantity, depth or breadth, coverage or understanding. A huge amount of information can be compressed into a relatively short amount of time, but the cost will be depth of understanding. A small amount of information can be defined, analyzed, and applied in a relatively large amount of time, but the cost will be coverage. Unfortunately, there is no easy way out of this dilemma, but we can manage our time better by using it for different purposes in the classroom.

In other words, blocks of time can be varied to suit your objectives: short blocks for lectures or stories, long blocks for experimentation and group

TEXTBOX 2.4

OFF THE WALLS

Time Marches On . . .

Read a story as fast as you can.
Read a story as slowly as you can.
Read a story as dramatically as you can.
Which has the greatest impact on students?
Which evokes the most responses?
Which is most satisfying to you?
Can time really be "saved?" Why or why not?

projects. Long or medium-sized amounts of time can be allotted for discussion, and relatively short bursts for quiet reflection, personal conversation, and self-directed study. Creative teachers can change the parameters to suit the assignments.

To build an atmosphere of inquiry and discovery, a classroom need not and probably should not be organized into equal time blocks of forty minutes each and every day. The main point is that time is flexible, as are materials and room arrangements, and can be varied for many different purposes and goals. Besides, a classroom in the age of electronics should be devoted to thinking on higher levels, not collecting facts readily available on the web.

BLENDING BEAUTY WITH ORDER

A room full of interesting things, machines, books, and "rich" corners is a place where a lot of thinking and working is going on, playful in tone, serious in purpose (Bergen 1988). Although this type of classroom is filled with artifacts and activities, there should be order and beauty in the way it is designed. The design is produced by both students and teachers, not teachers alone. Even the very youngest children, and certainly youth and adults, must have a say in shaping their environment. Teachers should seriously consider their suggestions. A cooperative and respectful spirit is built when all parties have a stake in how it looks and feels to them.

There is a second reason to listen to students: their views must have a place in the classroom. The alternative is to direct students to fulfill adult goals and imitate adult models, neither of which will tell you much about what is actually in their minds. For example, when the holidays come around, many elementary teachers ask students to help them create attractive exhibits or bulletin boards.

They display cutouts, pictures, photographs, or posters. Often, children and young adults simply imitate, even copy, established traditions: the image of a turkey or Pilgrims for Thanksgiving, Columbus's ships for Columbus Day, or outlines of Lincoln and Washington for Presidents' Day.

Why not allow students to devise their own interpretations of a holiday, perhaps centered on foods, symbols of government, ideas of democracy or exploration, or ethical values, creating somewhat unusual images and displays? Have a real discussion of holiday origins and meaning. Maybe some are not worth observing?

This type of self-expression permits creativity. Teachers can offer instruction about the event and discuss student insights. Let the students plan the bulletin board and escape from some of our timeworn (and sometimes quite inaccurate) traditions.

A TEACHER'S ROLE: WHO ARE YOU?

Guidance and direction are very different pedagogical functions. When you play the guide, you assist students with their ideas and projects. They have defined and initiated thinking. When you are the director, you are the authority whose commands shape the final product and student understanding.

This is not to say that commands are never to be uttered. There is a time for giving directions and enforcing discipline, but there is also a value to using students' ideas. Commands are excellent for moving smoothly toward a goal, a set objective, and deadlines. But the product won't afford much insight into student potential for creativity or deep observation.

Thus, your choice of roles depends on the context and subject of your lesson. To set up and maintain a productive and interesting classroom, students must have input. A student committee could be organized to make suggestions, with discussion and debate from the class. You could occasionally hand out a survey seeking written feedback, depending on the age and general capability of the class. Take a page from focus groups and marketing to determine what your "audience" thinks and wants.

You are still the director, but projecting a more democratic demeanor, right?

In general, creativity and play are generated in an atmosphere of open-ended goals and caring. With a solid foundation of observation, students can go off in directions they determine for themselves, suggested by materials available in a rich classroom environment. Creative teachers have arranged their classrooms and contents to evoke insightful active learning. Guiding students' work as enjoyable play, and play as enjoyable work, is accomplished through observation, fantasy, and perplexity, which build fascination. The problem or game sets the parameters, but the players build the strategy.

Together, creative teacher and students rise to new levels of understanding and insight.

TEXTBOX 2.5

OFF THE WALLS

Let's imagine ourselves in a desert riding a camel.

Who would we meet? Who would we be? Where are we in the world? What would we have for lunch? Where could we rest? How might we want to talk to our camel? Ask students to conduct a role-play in which they project themselves into a new place, a different environment, another culture, an alternative personality.

Ask them who they think did the best job of fantasizing another life, and why they believe it was fun to watch. Did they learn anything from the experience?

This is the beauty of play as a basis for creativity—inhibitions are released and imagination is given free rein. In this environment, work generates interest and becomes self-sustaining.

Better yet, when classroom play and work center on using raw data that strengthens intellectual skills and decision-making, the lines between work and play are blurred. This is an advantage for the teacher (or parent, or leader, or businessperson, etc.), who gains points for creating a positive atmosphere for play. Learners also win because they become enthusiastic about their studies as a kind of work that seems like play.

Walls disintegrate between the closed boxes that were once play and work, work and play, enhancing the desire to look outside the box and off the walls for new ideas.

REFERENCES

Anderson, L. W., and D. R. Krathwohl, eds. 2001. *A Taxonomy for Learning, Teaching, and Assessing: A Revision of Bloom's Taxonomy of Educational Objectives*, complete edition. New York: Longman.

Bergen, D., ed. 1988. *Play as a Medium for Learning and Development: A Handbook of Theory and Practice*. Portsmouth, NH: Heinemann Books.

Bloom, B. S. 1956. *Taxonomy of Educational Objectives, Handbook I: The Cognitive Domain*. New York: David McKay.

Bruner, J. 1983. "Play, Thought, and Language." *Peabody Journal of Education* 60 (3): 60–69.

Bruner, J. S., A. Jolly, and K. Sylvia. 1976. *Play: Its Role in Development and Evolution*. New York: Basic Books.

Carroll, Lewis. 1960. *The Annotated Alice*. New York: Bramhall House.

Conklin, J. 2006. *Wicked Problems and Social Complexity*. New York: John Wiley.

Dede, C. 2009. "Immersive Interfaces for Engagement and Learning." *Science* 323 (5910): 66–69.

Duffy, B. 1998. *Supporting Creativity and Imagination in the Early Years*. Philadelphia: Open University Press.

Fein, G. 1986. "The Play of Children" in *The Young Child at Play: Reviews of Research* (4), 7–14. Washington, D.C: National Association for Young Children.

Fredrickson, B. L. 2001. "The Role of Positive Emotions in Positive Psychology: The Broaden-and-Build Theory of Positive Emotions." *American Psychologist* 56 (3): 218–26.

Furth, H. G., and H. Wachs. 1974. *Thinking Goes to School.* New York: Oxford University Press.

Gilmore, J. A. 1985. "Play: A Special Behavior." In *Child's Play,* edited by R. E. Herron and B. Sutton-Smith. Malabar, FL: Kreiger & Sons.

Harrow, A. 1972. *A Taxonomy of Psychomotor Domain: A Guide for Developing Behavioral Objectives.* New York: David McKay.

King, N. 1982a. "School Uses of Materials Traditionally Associated with Children's Play." *Theory and Research in Social Education* 10 (3): 17–27.

———. 1982b. "Work and Play in the Classroom." *Social Education* 46 (2): 110–13.

Krathwohl, D. R., B. S. Bloom, and B. B. Masia. 1973. *Taxonomy of Educational Objectives, the Classification of Educational Goals. Handbook II: Affective Domain.* New York: David McKay.

Kreidler, W. J. 1984. *Creative Conflict Resolution.* Glenview, IL: Scott, Foresman.

Singer, J. L., and D. G. Singer. 1977. *Partners in Play.* New York: Harper & Row.

Sylva, K., J. S. Bruner, and P. Genova. 1976. "The Role of Play in Problem-Solving of Children 3–5 Years Old." In *Play: Its Role in Development and Evolution,* edited by J. S. Bruner, A. Jolly, and K. Sylva, 244–57. New York: Basic Books.

Creative Teaching and Learning

Theory and Practice

"The Stone Age didn't end because they ran out of stones."

—anonymous folk saying

"When a true genius appears in the world, you may know him by this sign, that the dunces are all in confederacy against him."

—Jonathan Swift, *Thoughts on Various Subjects*

INTRODUCTION

There are many descriptions of creativity. Although they differ widely, they have one aspect in common. Each of them describes the *process* of creativity, but most do not attempt to deal with its *causes*. In addition, most describe the entirety of creativity in its broadest sense. Few focus on educational applications. Some even argue that creativity cannot really be taught but grows out of the subconscious and is influenced by events that spark ideas and inventions (Campbell 1960, Simonton 1988). Most stress analytical processes, with creativity proceeding in a series of steps that usually begin with observation and the accumulation of knowledge.

FIGURE 3.1

One difference among theories of creativity involves its origin. Does it originate in underlying processes of thinking, or does it reside in the subconscious or the conscious, expressed as a sudden burst of ideas (Wertheimer 1945) or artistic expression (Vinacke, 1953)? We might call these the "stepwise theory" and the "gestalt theory." In the latter case, the creative process is hidden until we view the inner workings of the thinker, if he or she can or wishes to share that evolution with us. This theory contains a Zen-like view of insight as achievable by deep meditation and inner consciousness, by drifting away from data into a realm of transformational thinking.

Creative thinking is also seen as a building process that moves in neat steps toward an outcome (Weisberg 1993). Research, careful observation, and a considerable gestation period are necessary. Wallas (1926) proposed that the creative process entails four major steps or categories beginning with preparation, moving on to incubation and illumination (the birth of the idea, product, or action), and finally verification. Category systems have evolved from the earlier models and are usually more precise about the steps included in a creative endeavor. For example, Rossman (1931) proposed seven steps from observation through analysis to formulation, critique, the birth of a new idea, and finally experimentation. Osborn (1953), the inventor of the term "brainstorming," also developed a full-scale model of creative thinking in seven stages:

1. Orientation (identifying a problem)
2. Preparation (collecting relevant data)
3. Analysis (developing explanations and inferences)
4. Ideation (considering alternative ideas)
5. Incubation (relaxing and mulling over ideas)
6. Synthesis (fusing information and ideas into insights)
7. Evaluation (assessing insights against evidence and experimentation)

This looks surprisingly like that educational staple, Bloom's taxonomy of educational objectives, which ranks categories of cognition and affect by levels of difficulty and achievement.

In the 1980s and '90s, when there was a great deal of interest in teaching gifted and talented students, many notable attempts were made to reformulate these models. Among the more influential were efforts by Treffinger (Isaksen and Treffinger 1985) and Parnes (1992) to promote the creative problem-solving (CPS) model which was composed of six steps: 1) objective-finding, 2) fact-finding, 3) problem-finding, 4) idea-finding, 5) solution-finding, and 6) acceptance-finding.

These models fuse the scientific method with more open-ended thinking. They require "thinking outside the box." At about the same time, Barron (1988) offered categories that move from conception to gestation on to parturition, "bringing up the baby" by testing the developing idea. This work is similar to earlier models, but uses more playful terminology.

A particularly interesting model from this period was presented by Fritz (1991), "the process for creation," a cyclical view of creativity, which includes eight levels:

1. Conception
2. Vision
3. Situate in current reality
4. Take action
5. Adjust, learn, evaluate, re-adjust

6. Build momentum
7. Complete the project
8. Live with your creation

The thinking process begins with a search, creates ideas, tests them against the real world, adjusts, and moves on toward a finished project that leads to more new ideas and testing. Distinctions between conception and vision, or current reality and taking action, can be fuzzy, but Fritz is trying to help us think about novel ideas, products, and methods using current traditions and examples.

All of these models are based on human psychology, although some emphasize the subconscious, situational nature of invention, while others focus on the systematic, scientific process. Clearly, some see genius and inventiveness as welling up from deeper subconscious depths (the process of development being unclear even to the inventor) with others viewing creativity as subject to a rational process. Some, such as Csikszentmihalyi (1996), see personality as a key factor, while most view creativity as a product of complex interactions among learning, environment, personal opportunities, and insight.

Most of the models outlined suggest that there are systems for invention, but that the process itself may be hidden in the subconscious. This apparent dichotomy can be overcome by viewing creativity as the result of a complementary union. Systematic investigation supports "incubation," and incubation supports illumination followed by the seemingly sudden appearance of a new idea or invention. Thinking itself is hidden from view in a "black box" of the mind. Nonetheless, systematic steps were taken to achieve a novel idea.

These theories are fine, but how do they affect life in a classroom? First, theories aside, all creative geniuses have shared one common trait, deep knowledge of their field. Each was immersed in thinking about science or music, history or art. When the "new" painting or product or theory appeared in finished form, it was most likely the product of a deep developmental process. A great deal of time was spent on reflection or incubation, to use Wallas's terms. Even the inventors, in many cases, were unaware of how much work they did in their subconscious before achieving a fully developed form. Edison, for example, did not actually "invent" the lightbulb. His contribution was testing its practical value. Hundreds of experiments were involved. The end product could hardly be construed as a gestalt or an aha! Rather it was painstakingly achieved by systematic testing of small variations in components until there was one combination that worked reliably and safely. Edison's genius might be ascribed more to his systematic approach—and sales!

Jackson Pollock's dribble paintings seem effortless and random. They actually derive from more than one hundred years of abstract and expressionist experimentation. Pollock applied and experimented with these techniques and aesthetic theories in his own work. Thus, his improvisations did not come out of nowhere, although at the time they seemed quite certainly "off the walls" (or is that "on the walls?").

Perhaps both the "instant" or Zen view of breakthroughs in thinking and the more carefully organized steps toward creative products present essential truths about creativity. One can have sudden insights, but those insights are usually the products of considerable incubation, testing, and reconsideration. Somewhere along the way, ideas have been invented from a deep database or have evolved from significant predecessors.

CREATIVITY THEORY APPLIED TO INDIVIDUALS AND SOCIETY

Most of the people we worship as creative personalities are viewed as unique individuals, often termed "geniuses." Some of these chosen few evolve into globally recognized icons of intelligence and/or invention. Einstein, Mozart, Edison, Picasso, Gandhi, and perhaps someone like Bill Gates are seen as geniuses in their quite different fields of endeavor. No doubt they were or are highly creative. However, their products and ideas have been blown out of all proportion. Geniuses appear to spring from the head of Zeus, godlike, and usually male, somehow effortlessly producing or inventing wonderful ideas and things. The truth of creativity is much more complex, dependent on a wide variety of factors and luck.

Creativity is often defined in terms of a person's specialty and the unique quality of his or her inventions or ideas. How "success" was achieved is rarely investigated. One of the reasons for this lack of interest is the fear that we'll discover something that will detract from the geniuses' superior ratings. The genius was actually a fairly ordinary person in many ways, but subject to a set of influences that helped her or him blossom into the creative scientist, vibrant artist, or great leader in literature or media.

It usually turns out that each had special breaks of some kind. These include being a member of a highly creative or highly educated family; receiving an outstanding education from highly engaging and creative mentors; living in a social setting that encouraged change and out-of-the-box thinking; or receiving support from peers, parents, family, community, business, or government. How do these factors contribute?

Social Setting

Arieti (1976) argues that the social setting is *vital* to opening people up to new ideas and encouraging experimentation. He points out that people in restrictive and conformist social settings are not very productive either individually or in groups. However, in more open and innovative settings the same people turn out to be quite successful at making a living and often go on to great heights of creativity. He contrasts the suppression of Jews in eighteenth-century Poland with the achievements of Jewish emigrants to America as an example of success in new social settings.

In Poland, Jews were forced to live in designated areas, denied access to education, and were often quite poor. This forced many into an internal life in the community, one aided by a deep religious commitment. But there are few if any creative individuals in this group aside from religious figures.

As ideas of toleration and enlightenment grew, Poland and Eastern Europe began to change and open up. Jewish writers, scientists, leaders, and revolutionaries began to appear on the scene. Many fled persecution to France, England, and the US, where they found settings that specifically valued their skills and energy, encouraging scholarship and invention. Jews in the US entered the worlds of business, art, literature, education, music, and science in great numbers. From Einstein to Bernstein, they achieved what would not have been possible in their former social milieu.

Thus, individuals are shaped and changed by the social settings in which they find themselves. Creativity is socially defined, not simply the result of individual genetics or genius. Creative output depends greatly on prevailing cultures, economies, and openness to novel ideas, products, and practices.

As we all know, there are periods of history that seem to be very vibrant, such as the Renaissance in Italy. There is a burst of creative thinking because economic, political, and cultural conditions work together to support invention, but this may not be sustained. The economy may deteriorate, the political atmosphere may tighten, and the culture may harden, inhibiting creativity.

In schools, we are usually taught the history of creative periods, times of expansion and innovation. Who has learned the history of Italy after the Renaissance ends? Who spends time investigating ancient Athens after the fall of the Athenian empire? Why do we often view the Middle Ages as "dark" and uninviting in comparison to the Roman Empire or the Renaissance? What happened after the "golden age" of any one of a number of periods punctuating our textbooks? Periods of creative expression and political expansion are attractive. Dull, plodding, authoritarian, and traditional societies are viewed as uninteresting. Yet all contain creative people with the potential for creative expression.

As conditions change within a culture, what were once little-used or unrecognized skills and talents suddenly take on a new life and meaning. Society accepts or even embraces new forms. The result: a time of ferment and change, innovation and invention, later to be celebrated in textbooks.

CREATIVITY THEORY APPLIED TO TEACHING

Creative teaching can be viewed as a skill like acting (Sawyer 2004). One frequent analogy is teaching as performance. However, this comparison leaves open the question of whether that performance is scripted and tightly directed or improvised. Scripting implies that everything in a lesson has been laid out, questions and answers, with the outcome certain and determined. Improvisation implies that teachers and students, working collaboratively, shape and direct the lesson together (John-Steiner 2000).

Scripting is a form of direct instruction with teachers as actors and directors, pupils as audience (Timpson and Tobin 1982). Outcomes are predictable and lecturing is dominant, with questions coupled to answers that usually match and conform. A premium is placed on getting to a particular outcome or goal.

As we have seen in earlier chapters, a classroom that fosters creativity is by definition unscripted. It may be a performance, but the "director" is a shared role. In a creative classroom, students may play teacher, and teachers may act as students while pursuing a solution or debating an issue. Tracking and reflecting students' ideas count for considerably more than acting ability. Discussion and role-play dominate, rather than directed lecture, with a high degree of improvisation (Baker-Sennett and Matusov 1997). The audience (students) is active rather than passive, and sharing of ideas is part of this "constructivist" view. Shakespeare may be "improvised" with new costumes, settings, and interpretations, perhaps yielding new insights into meaning, or ruining the play entirely. So it is with creative teaching. Going outside the box may lead to an off-the-walls participatory performance. The experiment fails, but new insights are gained.

PERFORMANCE IN A CLASSROOM

What we are calling creative teaching is usually perceived as far more difficult to implement than traditional methods. Teachers worry about maintaining control and direction. In a creative classroom, outcomes are not guaranteed. Students may wander off the subject while improvising strategies and inventing ideas. Discourse can go in many directions and frequently seems unstructured or poorly structured. Thus many instructors are frightened of improvisation and imagination. They see these as wasting time and making assessment difficult and too risky. Knowledge acquired is the easiest to assess. A simple multiple-choice or fill-in exam will tell you whether students have "mastered" mercantilism or valence or phototropism. This mastery is easily attained by teacher as director. However, assessing skills development—analysis, inference, and insight—requires more sophisticated ways of evaluating student work.

IMPLEMENTING CREATIVITY

Every teacher, and everyone playing a teacher's role, from parents and friends (and students) to business leaders, can instruct in creative ways. Creative teaching ideas grow out of a combination of pragmatic philosophy and cognitive psychology that seeks to promote learners as active inquirers and investigators rather than passive receivers (Bruner 1973). Invention and discovery, not necessarily unique or original, are seen as vital to learning. Teachers influence, enlighten, and encourage individuals and groups to practice the skills of inquiry to achieve potential insights. From this perspective, students who rediscover the wheel *are* being insightful, although still inside the box. The replication of earlier discoveries and inventions is a way of learning material from the inside, much as the original inventor probably did. But this time, the students are practicing their own skills of investigation and drawing conclusions: if these agree quite closely with the original, then so much the better.

Students who come up with new ideas, new insights, or imaginative creations have gone beyond replication to invention. They are working outside the box. As Sawyer points out, "Creative teaching is disciplined improvisation because it always occurs within broad structures and frameworks" (2004, 13).

The *process* of discovery and invention is vitally important in creative teaching. As part of this process, it is extremely important that teachers (students, parents, leaders, etc.) do NOT supply ready-made answers. Reproduction of ideas and memories simply results in storage, not application, without much potential for extension or invention. A fully scripted lesson leaves little room for independent thought. Replication may be allowed, and perhaps modest insight, but jumping out of the box, much less off the walls, would be very disturbing and most likely disapproved of or suppressed. Teaching creatively may, therefore, be defined as loosely structuring a classroom setting, providing rich materials, and allowing learners to become comfortable taking risks and following their own paths to insight. Conversation will be increasingly unstructured, but can be disciplined as well. Teachers can fine-tune the amount of direction (discipline) needed, adapting to students' talents and interests. Creative teachers can also assess and adjust the degree of openness students can deal with in pursuing problems and thinking about issues (Cazden 2001).

Whether insight actually occurs, or occurs profusely, depends on factors that teachers often cannot control. But the message and expectations are the same: learning must have a knowledge base from which ideas grow and are tested *by the students*. Discussion may be initiated from any side: teachers' or students' or both; parents' and children's or both; entrepreneurs' and workers' or both. Collaboration brings forth richer discourse, shared discourse, then new permutations of ideas.

Motivation usually grows as teachers move toward inquiry, discovery, problem-finding and -solving. The locus of investigation has shifted to the learners. Student ideas are legitimated and valued, treated with recognition, and praised.

In an age of information overload and distraction, it is more important than ever that knowledge is used, tested, and played with, not simply memorized. After all, we have lovely machine memories with which to store data! Why waste time on storage when we could be actively engaged with problems, mysteries, discoveries, and, perhaps, just perhaps, inventions and insights?

Although the potential is limitless, the immediate goals for creative teaching can be quite modest. We cannot guarantee truly creative genius, but we can easily show increases in application of knowledge, deeper comprehension, richer explanation, all directed toward increased motivation and participation.

Improvisation can cut across all subjects and grades, all intellectual and physical levels, moving in stages from deep knowledge through incubation, from play to fully developed action. Teachers have to learn to work in and out of the box, cushioning the blows as they and students bounce off the walls.

CREATIVITY THEORY APPLIED TO LEARNING

Learning is a lot trickier than teaching. Teaching is public, open, and strategic, but learning is internal, ambiguous, and often idiosyncratic. The public role of teacher is usually active and clear, much like the role of business leader or entrepreneur. The role of student is often passive and accepting. Yet building creative potential is all about participation and productivity, not comfort and stasis. Learning is struggle.

No one can learn, acquiring knowledge and skills, without effort and interest (Dewey 1911). A dilemma for all teachers, particularly in this great electronic age, is that distractions are everywhere. The knowledge base is growing exponentially, creating a major challenge for learners who need some idea of how to find the knowledge they need and use it effectively. We are drowning in data (Bereiter 2002). And we are constantly diverted by incoming messages via phone, e-mail, or text. How can deep knowledge develop in a circus-like atmosphere of continuous information retrieval, telephone calls, and YouTube clips, all attended to simultaneously?

Creative teachers must understand how to select, sample, and transform these information streams into provocative curricula that engage students. And they must have strategies for sustaining and increasing learning (Brown and Edelson 2001). Conversation can be supported with data and structured by imaginative questions. Creative endeavor must be participatory, with students buying into each lesson as groups or individually (Sawyer 2003). Creative learning requires focus, concentration, dialogue, motivation, and participation. Ideally, learners and teachers and content form a triad contributing to growth and progress.

Discourse takes on new meaning in creative learning (Wertsch 1998). Students and teachers can observe thought patterns, noting breakthroughs to new levels of comprehension, analysis, and synthesis. They can assess each other's ideas rather than relying on an outside authority for verification. Talk becomes a measure of mental agility and inference, particularly if most of the talk is coming from students. As talk reaches new levels of thinking and contributions come from an increasing number of individuals and groups, discourse becomes less disciplined and more freeform. Ideas begin to flow more easily and explanations grow clearer; questioning takes on sharper edges. The box opens.

Learners must allow themselves the chance to be attentive. Curiosity also helps. Distractions must be minimized, replaced with an intense focus on the subject. Alas, this is easier said than done in most modern environments, including schools. The classroom, library, and study hall were places with the potential for calm inquiry, at least by the willing. Now, teachers try to drag students away from distractions.

Creative teachers try to jolt students out of complacent acceptance into a new world of skill development and insight. But the culture of school frequently demands conformity and tradition in both social and intellectual terms. Rigid and traditional teaching roles are usually not oriented toward challenge or change. When they are, many students feel surprised and uncomfortable. Why? Because tradition is comfort food, with participants knowing exactly where they are and what is expected. Copying notes from the blackboard (or SMARTboard) is an antiquated tradition. Yet many students (and teachers) see note-taking as learning and are satisfied with memorization.

Creative expression, by contrast, is open-ended and calls for risk-taking by both teacher and students. Thus, learning is at risk, torn between the pole of distraction and the pole of conformity (McLaren 1986). Somehow, somewhere, a balance must be struck between traditions, distractions, and innovations.

Innovative and imaginative thinking builds an atmosphere for discovery. Practicing skills of discovery and inquiry promotes insights into possible new applications and extensions of existing products, ideas, and technology. This ensures at least a basic cultural and social setting that values new ideas. However, as tradition takes hold corporations, schools, institutions, and yes, teachers, become more set in their ways, and the goals become merely reproductive rather than productive. To be fair, creativity is very difficult to sustain. Most of us, if successful, feel satisfied to rest on our laurels and let others do the difficult work of invention.

Schools often fall into a pattern, especially if their test results are good. Certain textbooks, methods, and organizational schemes are institutionalized. But if this goes on for decades, nothing changes within the box, although the outside world may have shifted dramatically. Companies and classrooms can lose their edge and become complacent. (In the case of classrooms, they may never have been near an edge.)

IMPLICATIONS FOR TEACHING

Teachers must assess the creative levels of learning encouraged by teaching methods and materials seeking insight into the black box of their students' minds. It is perhaps most difficult to ascertain what awakens and arouses interests, but without this knowledge, learning becomes a shadow play, a sham.

Individual students may have particular needs and problems that are not represented by a group average. Some have learning difficulties we may not know about; others have gifts that may not be realized in the classroom. Still more may be distracted by media, the ubiquitous cell phones, difficult emotions, or family issues. A certain portion of any class may view learning as irrelevant to their immediate needs and interests, refusing to participate or even pay attention.

With rote and tradition, students may be comfortable and quiet, but are divorced from actual learning, creative or traditional. All is predictable in that situation, but there is little to challenge anyone—a low-risk, low-return situation.

A class may defeat a teacher, even a strong, controlling, traditional teacher. Yet a more innovative and creative teacher has the potential to awaken and enliven students in general because of the unusual nature of creative instruction. The call for participation, productivity, self-expression, and invention work in a teacher's favor by drawing interest from all but the most catatonic. But there is a higher risk of unpredictable reactions and responses.

The challenge for creative learning is twofold: first, to build deep knowledge while developing inquiry skills; and second, to sustain a wide-enough variety of strategies and activities to stay fresh, exciting, and playful. The challenge for creative teaching is to walk a tightrope between direction and improvisation, between information overload and thoughtful inference. Above all, the goal of creative instruction is the production of ideas rather than the consumption of "facts."

Staying in the box is comforting while venturing outside is disconcerting, but creativity only occurs when deep knowledge meets big ideas and sparks fly off walls.

REFERENCES

Arieti, S. 1976. *Creativity: The Magical Synthesis*. New York: Basic Books.

Baker-Sennett, J., and E. Matusov. 1997. "School 'Performance': Improvisational Processes in Development and Education." In *Creativity in Performance*, edited by R. K. Sawyer, 197–212. Norwood, NJ: Ablex.

Barron, F. 1988. "Putting Creativity to Work." In *The Nature of Creativity*, edited by R. J. Sternberg. Cambridge, UK: Cambridge University Press.

Bereiter, C. 2002. *Education and Mind in the Knowledge Age*. Mahwah, NJ: Erlbaum.

Brown, M., and D. C. Edelson. April 2001. "Teaching by Design: Curriculum Design as a Lens on Instructional Practice." Paper presented at the annual meeting of the American Educational Research Association. Seattle, Washington.

Bruner, J. 1973. *Going beyond the Information Given*. New York: Norton.

Campbell, D. T. 1960. "Blind Variation and Selective Retention in Creative Thought as in Other Knowledge Processes." *Psychological Review* 67:380–400.

Cazden, C. B. 2001. *Classroom Discourse: The Language of Teaching and Learning*. 2nd ed. Portsmouth, NH: Heinemann.

Csikszentmihalyi, M. 1996. *Flow and the Psychology of Discovery and Invention*. New York: HarperCollins.

Dewey, J. 1911. *How We Think*. Boston: Heath.

Fritz, R. 1991. *Creating*. New York: Fawcett.

Isaksen, S. G., and D. J. Treffinger. 1985. *Creative Problem Solving: The Basic Course*. Buffalo, NY: Bearly Publishing.

John-Steiner, V. 2000. *Creative Collaboration*. New York: Oxford University Press.

McLaren, P. 1986. *Schooling as Ritual Performance: Towards a Political Economy of Educational Symbols and Gestures*. London: Routledge & Kegan Paul.

Osborn, A. 1953. *Applied Imagination*. New York: Charles Scribner.

Parnes, S. J. 1992 *Sourcebook for Creative Problem Solving.* Buffalo, NY: Creative Education Foundation Press.

Rossman, J. 1931. *The Psychology of the Inventor.* Washington, DC: Inventor's Publishing.

Sawyer, R. K. 2003. *Group Creativity: Music, Theater, Collaboration.* Mahwah, NJ: Erlbaum Publishers.

———. 2004. "Creative Teaching: Collaborative Discussion as Disciplined Improvisation." *Educational Researcher* 33 (2): 12–20.

Simonton, D. K. 1988. "Creativity, Leadership, and Chance." In *The Nature of Creativity,* edited by R. J. Sternberg. Cambridge, UK: Cambridge University Press.

Timpson, W., and D. N. Tobin. 1982. *Teaching as Performing: A Guide to Energizing Your Public Presentation.* Englewood Cliffs, NJ: Prentice Hall.

Vinacke, W. E. 1953. *The Psychology of Thinking.* New York: McGraw-Hill.

Wallas, G. 1926. *The Art of Thought.* New York: Harcourt Brace.

Weisberg, R. W. 1993. *Creativity: Beyond the Myth of Genius.* New York: W. H. Freeman.

Wertheimer, M. 1945. *Productive Thinking.* New York: Harper.

Wertsch, J. V. 1998. *Mind as Action.* New York: Oxford University Press.

4

Dimensions of Distraction and Invention

"It is obvious that anything that is gained with fatigue seems sweeter than what is acquired without any effort. The plain truth, since it is quickly understood with little difficulty, delights us and passes from the mind. But, in order that it may be more pleasing, because acquired with labor, and therefore better retained, the poets hide the truth beneath things apparently quite contrary to it. For that reason, they produce fables, rather than some other covering, because their beauty attracts those whom neither philosophical demonstrations nor persuasions would have been able to allure."

—Boccaccio, *The Life of Dante*, xxii

"Oh, come on teach, *just tell* it to me, OK?"

—recorded May 2011 in a New York middle school

CREATIVITY AND CONFORMITY: AN ECOLOGICAL PERSPECTIVE

Teaching creatively occurs in a complex milieu where there are many competing forces. These forces may reinforce and sustain inventiveness, or distract from and inhibit new ideas and approaches. These forces range from the macrocosmic to the microcosmic—the values and expectations of the

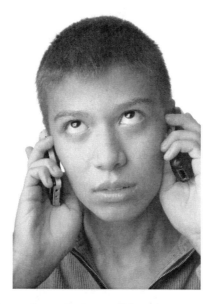

FIGURE 4.1

nation (even the world) down through those of the community, school, and individual classroom (Bronfenbrenner 1979).

The goals of curriculum materials and instructional processes derived from these influences are often inconsistent and conflicting. The result is a diminution of both teacher effectiveness and student performance. Despite the reform program in the US, widespread teaching to the tests, and cheating, scores on national assessments have only improved marginally for decades. Since 1971, reading and math scores improved a bit for nine-year-olds, a little less for thirteen-year-olds, and not at all for high school seniors (Stedman 2009).

We need to rethink *the total environment* in which teaching and learning take place and develop an ecological model of the creative classroom (Barab and Roth 2006). This social setting is affected at two levels, the microcosmic and macrocosmic. The macrocosm is the larger context imposed by the state of the world and its influence on states and societies, and groups across the globe. The microcosm, such as a school or family, is the local, personal, insider view of macrocosm and its effects. Each may vary considerably, allowing a lesser or greater range of freedom to inquire that supports or hinders practice and experimentation.

Our little schools and classrooms reside within larger social units. Even the largest schools represent no more than a small town's worth of folks. Some are just villages or hamlets. All, however, are subject to local customs, administrations, rules, mores, supply lines, and curricular demands. Some of these come from outside and above: the federal government, local influences, parents and businesses, and religious groups. Thus, the macrocosm impacts the microcosm, but each microcosm also has a unique life of its own.

Within the microcosm that begins when we walk through a school door is a small town or village with its own peculiar history, population, customs, and rules. This history and population meld into a social, political, and cultural atmosphere that is an ecological system. School administrations provide leadership (we hope), teachers provide knowledge and skills, students provide an audience, and staff provide food, warmth, sports, security, and maintenance. Each contributor gives her or his own little bit of character and value to the overall ecology. A culture develops that promotes or inhibits the mental health of its inhabitants. This adds up to a microcosm that works to promote or inhibit creative, outside-the-box, or off-the-walls teaching (Wenger 1998).

In some schools, students are there for fun or to make trouble. They don't really want to learn much of anything. They are waiting for lunch or to meet their friends. In other schools, the students are serious about learning for good or bad reasons and work hard to acquire knowledge. These guys might even read books on their own, without teacher coercion. Clearly, student culture will have a significant effect on the microcosm.

Teachers are also very important, as they work directly with students, providing knowledge and skills within the context of teaching, lending character to the microcosm that is the school. Most of us still remember teachers we loved or hated, though we may have forgotten the curriculum.

How teachers interpret and implement the curriculum is crucial for promoting learning, particularly more creative brands of learning. The microcosmic mix of teachers, students, leaders, and materials makes up a matrix of forces that eventually produces satisfying or frustrating results. However, these results—meaning deep learning, not just test scores—are often misunderstood until much later in the game.

In any ecosystem, including a school, a good deal of time is needed to digest, process, and synthesize knowledge into a pattern of improvement or decline. You can't get results overnight. The current obsession with test scores and "reform" often overlooks the overall ecology of change within the microcosm of a school, much less the macrocosm of society. There must be *real changes, an investment in training, content, and methods,* for results to improve, at least from a creative point of view. Doing more of the same will result in more of the same—scores stable and going nowhere, and certainly not up.

Where's the motivation?

Each cosmos influences attitudes, feelings, and knowledge acquisition. Each creates perceptions about content, process, and value. How we perceive our situations is vital to how we behave as teachers or learners or administrators, and it creates a sense of health or anxiety about the world we live in (Schutz and Luckmann 1973). This might be called a phenomenological or "felt" view of classrooms and schools, as well as society and the world. Within the school microcosm, feelings about a setting may work greatly in favor of vibrant, inquiring classrooms, or of dull, pedantic classrooms. Attitudes yield a "phenomenon" or perception of growth (we are excited!), status quo (we are stuck!), or decline (we are failing!).

Thus, a school's ecology may or may not communicate approval of intellectual, cultural, or physical challenge. There are satisfying results in art classes, sports, science projects, and writing. Or the combination of factors may produce a sense of cynicism toward teaching and learning. Cynicism and depression tend to grow from lack of administrative support, poor student cooperation, and teacher exhaustion and burnout. Each ecological setting produces its own view of life in the microcosm, its own judgments on the community (Wenger 1998). School can be warm and comforting, protective, stimulating, or prison-like, across a phenomenological range.

Perceptions of the demands of the greater world are also seen through a local lens. Microcosm and macrocosm may reinforce and support each other or they may work at cross-purposes. This agreement or lack thereof will shape how educational results are viewed and how learning outcomes are perceived. These are potentially serious issues that influence the way populations see schools, teachers, and students. Who gets the blame and how teachers are viewed become key factors in promoting or inhibiting creative teaching.

When teachers are respected and valued, the school's curriculum is more creative. In places that support teachers in making their own professional choices, there are usually more subject choices, better extracurricular programs, and more innovation. Communities that see teachers as unsuccessful slackers tend to impose a uniform curriculum (and low pay) that allows little room for negotiation or innovation.

The tension between the mores of the community and the demand for rapid development of human capital presents huge issues for creative teaching. Many communities appear to want strict adherence to traditions as well as attainment of personal success. They want conformity and creativity, without seeing the contradictions inherent in their goals. Do we want knowledgeable young citizens, skillful learners, and activists? Or is our goal good workers drawn from groups of nicely docile students?

Of course, we want it all, but alas, creativity and conformity do not peacefully co-exist. When we think about teaching and learning creatively, conformity and tradition vs. innovation and exuberance is at the root of our dilemma. We have to choose among building a vibrant educational ecosystem, remaining stuck, or falling prey to an industrial assembly-line model.

ENCOMPASSING CIRCLES OF INFLUENCE

While creative teaching and learning occur in a microcosm, it is the macrocosm that provides the setting and support. World conditions influence creative opportunities. Regional and national conditions create cultural values and educational/economic opportunities. A particular community, with a population more or less supportive of education and innovation, sets the tone for experimentation or conformity. But investment is usually stimulated nationally. A school resides within these external rings, taking in values, opportunities, demands, and learners. A cohort of teachers of many subjects is hired to present a body of knowledge that may be set in stone or negotiable.

That is not to say that the society alone defines an individual community or that the community alone determines the goals and performance of a school. Within each school there is a unique mix of creative, ordinary, and uncreative teachers, each going his or her own way. Schools and even individual teachers may provide more than the community expected, or even wanted, although this requires a supportive school administration. If the juices of invention are flowing, there is a happy confluence of interest and support. If the juices of inhibition dominate, the innovative and unusual will drown.

THE ECOLOGY OF EDUCATION

Once the classroom door is closed, it is the teacher who makes the final, cosmic decisions. Each teacher has a unique personality with both talents and weaknesses. Whatever is affecting that person can influence levels of creativeness (Barab and Roth 2006). A happy state, a playful situation, praise and rewards, personal recognition, all usually promote creative learning. Intense interest, a passion for experimentation, and the freedom to pursue ideas also build the atmosphere for creative teaching and learning.

A second, critical, element in this ecological system is the physical setting. An active, inquisitive, vibrant classroom where students are encouraged to pursue many and varied avenues of interest usually bolsters creativity. A rich array of materials, objects, and activities opens minds to alternative paths to knowledge, encouraging hands-on experimentation.

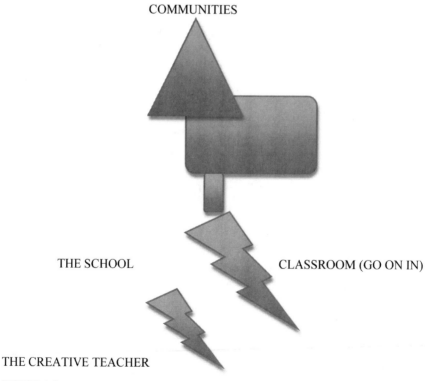

COMMUNITIES

THE SCHOOL

CLASSROOM (GO ON IN)

THE CREATIVE TEACHER

FIGURE 4.2

Students eager for inquiry play into a teacher's strengths, creating harmony. Mental health improves for all. Teachers want to spend time with a class that is receptive, not so much with a class that is obstreperous. If there are too many discipline problems in a classroom, teachers will opt for regimentation and may turn to punishment. Creative potential will ebb on both sides. Unfortunately, regimented classrooms where discipline and organization are paramount may provide order and information, but little or nothing in the way of creativity. Teachers encouraging creativity demand a degree of looseness and openness that may not be conducive to perfect discipline, but yields a lot of ideas.

The school itself is a vital component in our educational ecology. A school may praise student (and teacher) accomplishments and promote a rich variety of extracurricular activities, providing recognition for outstanding effort. In contrast, repressive and poor schools exuding control and conformity as the prevailing ethos will find it very difficult to promote and sustain basic interest, much less creative attainment.

Encompassing these factors is the society as a whole. A creative society encourages innovation in all spheres, from business to health and even education. It offers opportunities for personal growth. Freedom of expression and toleration of alternative viewpoints are expected.

Thus, each circle affects individuals, classrooms, schools, and the social order, setting the scene for creative teaching and learning, or not. Ideas are the coin of the realm in creativity rather than data collection. But ideas need to be discussed and reflected on, growing apace as knowledge expands and deepens. Ultimately, student creativity comes from within, after teacher, school, and social influences converge. As their self-confidence develops, the students will begin to "run with the ball" by themselves.

PERSONAL

On the personal level, as a teacher, your mood is crucial to creativity. Of course, you also have to buy into a philosophy of teaching that promotes problem-finding and problem-solving. Once in, you should consider what experiences will increase students' attention and sense of accomplishment and satisfaction. At least four factors play key roles in promoting attention and also give the teacher the opportunity to "do" theater:

1) playfulness, 2) drama, 3) rapport, and 4) choice of materials.

Playfulness communicates a sense of openness and draws students in. Drama offers spectacle, emotions, a feeling of being part of a stage show. Call on students to play parts in the learning drama. Ask them to act out lessons, write a script and perform what happened at Valley Forge, declaim at a poetry slam, build and test a landform map made with Play-Doh, or paint a picture blindfolded.

Rapport is how teachers relate to students on a personal/human level. It requires empathy and a willingness to allow students a say in learning. Why not ask students to assess the curriculum and its method of presentation? Then select materials based on student responses that show respect for their interests.

Curricula, the materials for instruction, continually need redesign to suit a modern, technologically savvy audience. That doesn't mean SMARTboards and DVDs necessarily, but materials, even if they're printed, that engage the skills of students. If materials are chosen carefully, with practice students should be asking questions about content and word selection by the fifth line of a document. When viewing an image, they ask for a closer look at details. In a science demonstration, participation begins immediately. But materials must be chosen to draw immediate attention and sustain interest.

A creative teacher has to clearly appreciate and assess a class, offering materials just a bit advanced for them. These more difficult materials must intrigue and stir student interest, but not frustrate them—Vygotsky's "zone of proximal development" (Vygotsky 1978).

There are a few key rules for creating or choosing provocative materials.

First, materials must not be oversimplified. Where possible, use "authentic" materials, actual speeches or documents pertaining to the subject.

Second, materials should be dramatic, colorful, imaginative, and, above all, provocative.

Third, materials ought to be rich in message and meaning, symbols and signs.

Fourth, materials should appeal to students' natural curiosity; they should raise questions but not answer them.

Fifth, and last, materials should evoke feelings and emotions, drawing students out of a state of apathy.

Alas, despite all of our postmodern electronic media, most materials are presented in the most pedestrian manner conceivable. If students are just sponges absorbing data, how can they be creative? Materials should invite active participation, not phony interactivity. Otherwise, teachers are competing with cell phones, computers, TVs, other students, and the outside world. But they are still inside a box!

As personal attention is lost, students wander off, and meaningful learning diminishes to the vanishing point.

AN AGE OF ELECTRONICS

One of the primary satisfactions of life in the new electronic age is the nearly instant availability of information (Dede 2009).

We have wonderful gadgets that allow us to communicate with others, retrieve data, store information, analyze problems, and even invent new ideas and products. Theoretically, the new electronic age makes it so easy to be inventive and creative that all can take advantage of the situation and go outside the boxes we live in. There is a general sense of optimism about computers and their capabilities. Electronics certainly make us more efficient and give us easy access to continually increasing reams of data. But what to do with it all is an open question.

There are online resources that teach, inform, and entertain, as well as lie and upset us. We can make an instant stock purchase, check our finances online, push buttons to buy almost anything we want, learn how to murder bedbugs, and send messages by e-mail, mail, telephone, outer space, cloud formations, and so on. The speed and clarity of the new channels of communication and their potential for learning are dizzying. The Net enables research, data accumulation, and analysis of results in amounts and at speeds unthinkable just a few decades ago. Small wonder we feel euphoric about the web!

Yet the technology boom has also created new issues and problems for teaching and learning. In fact, schools themselves, as traditionally configured, are basically holdovers from an earlier time and place. They descend from an industrial model whose base is rapidly disintegrating, leaving us with a "rust belt" of stale curricula. Oddly, although most schools have embraced technology by investing heavily in computers, LCD projectors, SMARTboards, and the like, they don't seem to know how to handle new equipment creatively. Many schools, including a few written up in national newspapers and journals, have every technology at their fingertips, yet their students' performance remains stagnant. Schools tend to either dismiss or overlook this problem. Faith in technological progress blinds educators to the essentially organic nature of learning. People, especially children, are not machines. We learn in frustratingly personal ways at frustratingly different paces. Particularly in the early years, children learn best from experience and hands-on exploration (Brophy 1997).

Computers may actually distract from this process. Instead of direct, hands-on contact with materials, we are creating "virtual" worlds for passive learning.

In addition, as long as we hang on to the industrial model of education, we will continue to focus on learning as knowledge accumulation. Teachers are presenters, conveyors, tellers, and judges. Despite access to nearly unlimited quantities of data, we are still treating students as human sponges and teachers as sources of as much information as they can absorb.

Electronic systems can stimulate and sustain creative thinking, but they are seldom used for such purposes by schools. Schools do not trust electronic media to deliver the goods in forms they do best, through games, simulations, videos, and web searches. Basically schools, and teachers, employ technology to promote acquisition of knowledge, hence the popularity of PowerPoint presentations, which are basically board notes in an electronic format, albeit sometimes with pictures and music.

Many of these lessons are supplemented with textbook exercises and worksheets, culminating in a multiple-choice examination. This series of redundancies may promote knowledge accumulation, but it does little to engender creativity. In addition, we are asking students to memorize information that is easily and quickly accessible, a waste of time.

Traditions die hard, even in changing atmospheres, even when they were *never* terribly successful. To make a real difference in students' lives and learning, teachers need to experiment with methods and materials that take advantage of the vast resources available. Teachers also need to rethink their primary goals: knowledge or skills, data acquisition or critical thinking, passive absorption or active engagement. Of course, these are polar opposites and most schools and teachers are in-between, pursuing several, sometimes contradictory, goals.

Why do we need to rethink our goals? Because right now, as an educational system, we are more or less stuck. Testing on local, state, and national levels indicates little or no progress. Educational reformers have put their time and money into rearranging schools and evaluating teachers and students, while leaving content and pedagogy virtually the same. Even with computers, SMARTboards, and iPads, technology is simply used to reproduce the same failed approaches.

Students need to learn how to find, organize, and judge data, memorizing only a small portion as needed. It would also be helpful if we could specify what it is we want students to learn, both in terms of knowledge and skills.

The new national common core standards could be helpful in this context, particularly if they are universally adopted, but much training and materials are still needed for implementation.

AN OVERDOSE OF MESSAGES

The vast flow of information is astounding and satisfying, but also over-whelming (Lankshear and Knobel 2006). Given this availability, a creative teacher must also be a selective teacher. In every subject, more data are available than can be mastered in several lifetimes. And a good deal of what is available may be useless or fraudulent.

So we must choose which messages to share with students, and these should be carefully selected for attractiveness, richness, and intellectual stimulation. In other words, teachers need to preview sites, texts, and materials to maximize their value and impact. The materials chosen should entertain and engage simultaneously, provoke lots of questions and ideas, and spark interest and sustain investigation.

Going to a website and tooling around without any clear objectives can be frustrating. And not all sites are born equal. Some are much better organized than others, with guidelines, suggested lessons, focused questions, and clear categories. Others are great masses of wonderful data that would require months to use for a few classroom presentations. It's best to start with a clear idea of what you want/need. Otherwise, you'll waste a great deal of time browsing. You need to come up with questions and skills that will guide your investigations: what do you want students to know and be able to do? Questions ought to be thought-provoking and open to a variety of responses.

Use "big ideas" to help students select and organize information. They provide a way of classifying knowledge as it grows and is added to a student's repertory. Each discipline has several key ideas that guide thinking. New and old information can be grouped and regrouped. For example, the idea of evolution in science (or in other fields) can be used to organize many kinds of data: from morphology, fossils, and the environment to social change and the big bang theory, or art and music.

Teachers can teach students how to learn rather than what to learn. Stress learning skills rather than information. In effect, teach students how to research, analyze, and evaluate data sets. Students will learn how to categorize problems and create solutions using investigative methods they develop along the way. Students will become detectives who ask questions and seek clues to eventually create comprehensive or specific answers. Whoever truly understands and can apply basic principles to "number facts" will find solving new math problems quite easy.

Given the superabundance of information, be choosy. But be choosy based on solid criteria that guide data collection and analysis. After a "guided" study, students have a better grasp of methods for investigation in a discipline. Messages begin to make sense and fall into groupings. Details stand out as meaningful rather than add to the confusion. Theories and explanations emerge as reasonable and can be checked against new arguments and proposals.

A sense of self-confidence develops, bolstering problem-solving. Liberated from the tyranny of too much information, we can select examples that are likely to be important and meaningful, open to new developments and ideas.

ASKING ABOUT MULTITASKING

Multitasking is doing several things at the same time. We believe in it, even though several studies indicate that it's impossible (Greenhow, Robelia, and Hughes 2009). In some ways, the myth and reality collide at a classroom door. In a typical classroom, there may be messages coming in from the administration, other colleagues, and students.

While a teacher is trying to get a lesson under way, students are arriving late and bells are ringing, with now and then a fire drill, assembly, or screaming match adding to the diversions. Meanwhile, a bee may wander in through an open window, throwing students into mock or real panic. Ambulances or fire engines may go by, drowning out conversation. The principal or department head may arrive for an observation.

These common disorders are bad enough. Add to them the much more sophisticated distractions of technological life. Where students once passed notes, daydreamed, or drew pictures on the desk, they now have mobile phones (yes, most school don't allow these, ha ha) and mini-computers or game consoles.

Messaging, texting, and online searches may be going on while a lesson is in progress, relating to or independent of the topic. In many classrooms, computers, TVs, or SMARTboards may actually divert attention from the learning process. Little Johnny and Mary wander off on tangents, getting interested in all that rich, lovely, entertaining data, and clean forget the goal of their work. It's easy to be distracted because there is too much going on, too much available.

Teachers compound the problem by showing a whole film or TV program without advance organizers, questions, or pauses for comments and inquiries, a formula for distraction, not attention. Of course, much depends on the nature and size of the film. A dramatic and startling movie will hold students' attention for two hours, if you have that much time, but you probably do not.

As the film moves along, a teacher can easily lose track of its effects on learners. What are they getting out of it? Are they in tune with the reasons you chose it in the first place? Are they really paying attention? How are they analyzing and learning from the film? Are they looking at their cell phones under the desks? Do they have earphones in? Are they doing homework during the movie? Taking notes?

Is doing a number of things at the same time a detriment or a supplement to the film?

Multitasking is very much with us in our age of computers and cell phones (also now approaching computer status). And this leaves out older forms of attention deflectors like people watching, flirting, and gossiping. We are left with worrying about how to help students focus on the worthwhile. But is the worthwhile as we see it, as they see it, or as the official curriculum enshrines it?

Multitasking is made possible by all the devices that extend our intellectual and communication skills, but these may also produce a loss of focus on a main objective. Learning as a whole becomes diluted and fuzzy, fragmented rather than sharp and propelling. Many competing goals combined with many competing messages may result in much greater intake, but also in much less understanding. Multitasking may not be multi-asking.

STUCK IN A BOX

Doing the same material over and over can lead to *seeking* distraction. Boredom in a classroom pushes restless minds to other endeavors: games, play, daydreaming, messaging, or just fooling around.

If lessons follow the same model, day-by-day, week-by-week, students will know when to opt out without being caught, and this includes repetitious electronic presentations. How many of you have been subjected to PowerPoint presentations that were accompanied by a printed version of the displayed text, yet still forced you to sit and watch the screen while the "presenter" read the text out loud? How many readers have done the same thing in a classroom?

Creative teachers vary lessons, pacing, strategies, materials, and topics, frequently surprising students with new and dramatic information. They engage students' emotions, movement, and cognitive capacities, perhaps all at the same time. Imagination should be built into the content and methodology consistently and regularly, a normal part of everyday creativity (Richards 2009).

Appreciation for a subject grows out of the attempt to attach students emotionally as well as cognitively to content and process.

VIRTUAL REALITY: INVENTIONS AND FABRICATIONS

The computer age has not only overwhelmed us with vast quantities of information, it has also blurred the line between fantasy and reality (DeGennaro 2008). We are subjected to vampire presidents, infomercials that blend information and a sales pitch, "reality" TV that gives the appearance of reality with the staging of classical drama. Docudramas combine what really happened with attractive people who are much easier on the eye. We've even invented words for these hybrids, among them "virtual reality." "Where do these fit in a classroom?" should be the question for teachers and learners.

Fiction films, while "based on fact," usually have better story lines, far superior actresses and actors, and much larger budgets than the more accurate documentary productions from history or science channels. Fabrications, whole or partial, erode the factual content that may indeed seem boring on the surface. The whole manner of presentation is attractive and appealing in comparison to a document or painting that, as one student told me recently, "just lays there."

Moving images, joined with quick action, outsized characters, and engaging sound or music, may jolt many students out of complacency, but at a cost. That cost is obscuring the difference between reality and fabrication.

However, this blurring of lines actually provides teachers with wonderful opportunities to creatively draw students into investigations that sort reality from invention. Students can be challenged to distinguish how the authors/directors/artists manipulated story lines and characters. With intelligence and a modicum of study, the blurred line may be turned against itself and made into a mystery to solve: What is true? And for the bolder: What is truth and is truth truly mightier than fiction? For the still bolder: Why am I being manipulated into believing something I may not want to believe?

Making students conscious of the methods used to present information is actually one of the most powerful and useful gifts a teacher can give. It yields insights not only into subjects but also into our own roles as processors of information. Consider the information available about global warming—real, combined, and simply made up. Students can evaluate the evidence as well as use it to debate the issue. In fact, the process of evaluating sources may itself provoke some lively discussion.

Adding information, analysis, findings, and conflicting views may keep the discussion going for a very long time. In the process, a great deal of science and history, not to mention an evaluation of social issues, may spring from what could have been a rather dull polemical presentation on weather patterns or species extinction. Cascades of information become a series of probing questions about the nature of knowledge.

In some fields, like literature and art, fabrication is a way of life. The fabrication itself is treasured and often produces deep emotion. We greatly value art, music, and literature that impact our souls though we know (at least at the subconscious level) that they have been invented. Theater, TV, or literary characters may be better than "the real thing," and far more valued. "Edutainment" and "docudrama," while blurring differences between reality and fantasy, give teachers a chance to be creative, posing questions and designing activities to "test for truth."

CONCLUSION

The new world of education, within the new world of the web, within the global "net," presents perhaps too many opportunities to be consumers and too few to be producers. Answering messages is important, and fun, because it appeals to our narcissism. We are the focus of attention. However, if we respond to all communications, there will be little time left for serious study, much less creative response and invention. Creative thinking requires that we have some idea of what is sought. There must be a fairly well-defined problem to solve or task to complete using skills that have been honed and practiced in a supportive atmosphere.

The most valuable skills emerging in the modern world of web-based research and teaching are deeply contradictory. On one side we have built vast storehouses of data, whether fantasy or reality, easily manipulated, revised, arranged, and housed on our computers or in the "cloud." We have access to almost limitless fields of inquiry.

On the other side, much of the available data may be unreliable. We are dazzled by discoveries, and the amounts and the distortions overload our senses and intellects. Data are fragmented and overlaid with sales pitches and entertaining quips or features, purposely designed to distract us. Like Harrison Bergeron, protagonist of a Kurt Vonnegut story, all of us are wearing buzzers and machines to dull our senses, but ours are self-imposed (Vonnegut 1961).

More than ever, it is critical thinking skills that help us to focus, model, and theorize, cut through and make sense of all the "stuff" collected. These skills help us to sort out and translate knowledge that actually helps us solve problems rather than become diverted by meaningless play. But these skills are not easily acquired. They must be practiced and honed with the guidance of creative teachers. The students must cooperate, buying into lessons. Without feeling, action, and attention, deep knowledge will not develop. The vast treasures of the web, and of the ages, will be beyond the grasp of distracted students.

Thus as education, including instruction, enters the much-touted Age of Electronics, we are faced with the need for deep reflection on our future. Are live teachers necessary anymore, or can we be offered canned on YouTube? If canned like tuna, how long is our shelf life? And were there any bugs, errors, or contaminants when the canning took place?

There are some who seek to replace teachers with a master computer. Perhaps every child can be replaced with a smaller computer plugged into this mommy machine. This could save a lot of money and each computer could be personally adapted to individual needs attended by differentiated instruction. But if this happens, who will be left to raise the questions that need to be asked? Who would offer empathy with student problems and fine-tune the curriculum to match the audience? Who would care?

Before an electronic future comes to pass, let's do humankind a favor and ask a few of the big questions.

Key Questions for Creative Classrooms of the Future
1. Is technology alone enough to guarantee improved learning?
2. Do the advantages of technology outweigh the distractions?
3. Which settings have the largest number of distractions: classrooms, schools, businesses, or government?
4. What learning has the greatest value: personal, educational, physical, or social?
5. Do new technologies and innovative methods of presentation engage the intellect, emotions, and motor skills?
6. Are learners taught how to verify and corroborate information? Do they have a healthy skepticism toward sources?
7. Do students buy into learning higher-order skills as well as gleaning accurate knowledge and cleaning out the questionable?
8. Are teachers prepared to use technology to enhance thinking and feeling, acting and motor skills?
9. Are teachers evolving a philosophy and psychology of technological innovation or is technology imposed on the classroom?
10. How are electronic databases and websites used? Are they for accessing and collecting data or for investigating, providing insights, drawing inferences, critical questioning?
11. What is the shape of things to come: computers learning from other computers, work as entertainment, play as reality, or_____?

Feel free to add your own "future query" to this list and let's move on to classroom examples of creative teaching and learning. And, please, try to avoid all distractions while continuing to read this book. Thank you so much.

REFERENCES

Barab, S. A., and J. A. Plucker. 2002. "Smart People or Smart Contexts? Cognition, Ability, and Talent Development, in an Age of Situated Approaches to Knowing and Learning." *Educational Psychologist* 37:165–82.

Barab, S. A., and W.-M. Roth. 2006. "Curriculum-Based Ecosystems: Supporting Knowledge from an Ecological Perspective." *Educational Researcher* 35 (5): 3–13.

Bronfenbrenner, U. 1979. *The Ecology of Human Development.* Cambridge, MA: Harvard University Press.

Brophy, J. 1997. *Motivating Students to Learn.* Guilford, CT: McGraw-Hill.

Dede, C. 2009. "Technologies That Facilitate Generating Knowledge and Possibly Wisdom." *Educational Researcher* 38 (4): 260–63.

DeGennaro, D. 2008. "Learning Designs: An Analysis of Youth-Initiated Technology Use." 41 (1): 1–20.

Greenhow, C., B. Robelia, and J. Hughes. 2009. "Learning, Teaching, and Scholarship in a Digital Age." *Educational Researcher* 38 (4): 24659.

Lankshear, C., and M. Knobel. 2006. *New Literacies: Everyday Practices and Classroom Learning.* Maidenhead, UK: Open University Press.

Richards, R., ed. 2009. *Everyday Creativity and New Views of Human Nature: Psychological, Social, and Spiritual Perspectives.* Washington, DC: American Psychological Association.

Schutz, A., and T. Luckmann. 1973. *The Structures of the Life-World.* Evanston, IL: Northwestern University Press.

Stedman, L. C. 2009. "Long Term Trends in NAEP Reading and Math Assessments: A Review of Its Transformation, Use, and Findings." A paper prepared for the NAEP Governing Board. Washington, D.C.: National Assessment for Educational Progress/U.S. Department of Education.

Vonnegut, K. October 1961. "Harrison Bergeron." *Magazine of Fantasy and Science Fiction*, republished in *Welcome to the Monkey House.* 1968. New York: Dell Books.

Vygotsky, L. S. 1978. *Mind in Society: The Development of Higher Psychological Processes.* Chapter 6, "Interaction between Learning and Development Processes," 79–91. Cambridge, MA: Harvard University Press.

Wenger, E. 1998. *Communities of Practice: Learning, Meaning, and Identity.* Cambridge, UK: Cambridge University Press.

5

Engines for Creative Teaching

"We all operate in two contrasting modes, which might be called open and closed. The open mode is more relaxed, more receptive, more exploratory, more democratic, more playful and more humorous. The closed mode is the tighter, more rigid, more hierarchical, more tunnel-vision-ed. Most people, unfortunately, spend most of their time in the closed mode. Not that the closed mode cannot be helpful. If you are leaping a ravine, the moment of takeoff is a bad time for considering alternative strategies. When you charge the enemy machine-gun post, don't waste energy trying to see the funny side of it. Do it in the 'closed' mode. But the moment the action is over, try to return to the 'open' mode—to open your mind again to all the feedback from our action that enables us to tell whether the action has been successful, or whether further action is need to improve on what we have done. In other words, we must return to the open mode, because in that mode we are the most aware, most receptive, most creative, and therefore at our most intelligent."

—John Cleese, TV comedian best known as a star of *Monty Python's Flying Circus*

"Following the rules and protecting the regulations is binding oneself without rope."

—Robert Aitken, *The Gateless Barrier: The Wu-Men Kuan (Mumonkan)*

INTRODUCTION

Creativity is a powerful and easy step forward in learning because learners are direct interpreters of evidence and producers of ideas (Amabile 1983). However, creativity is also difficult because it requires a combination of skills: a balance between imagination, knowledge, and feelings (Sternberg 1997). This fusion of skills is not easily achieved in most classrooms. Schools generally focus on the acquisition of knowledge because that is most easily delivered and measured.

Further, the public seems to accept test scores as proof of learning. This is knowledge by consumption, however, not "deep" knowledge achieved by struggling with problems. It is surface knowledge, easily revealed when a teacher asks a few higher-order, tough questions. Psychological studies have clearly demonstrated that large amounts of what look to the learner like random facts are easily forgotten (Baddeley 1997). If information isn't meaningful, the mind soon loses both the knowledge and the interest in keeping it alive, half or more lost after the first day (Schacter 2001)!

Measuring reasoning skills and inference is a bit more difficult, but techniques have long been available to do so, such as document-based questions (DBQs) and various forms of essays. Advanced Placement (AP) examinations are models of advanced test-making as well as test-taking, but are usually reserved for elite students. So, despite the fact that higher-order cognition is somewhat more difficult to assess than factual knowledge, test makers have devised ways of judging the reasoning processes in the little black boxes of our minds.

Higher-order thinking requires more effort on the part of both teachers and students (Byrnes 2001). Measuring creativity, the level we want to achieve, presents a mixed set of problems. Feelings and attitudes are actually easy to measure, but we tend to ignore them in a school setting. How often do we ask students to assess teaching methods and materials, or themselves, for that matter?

Imagination, innovation, and invention are extremely difficult to measure because our definitions disagree. Insight demands going beyond the data given to higher levels of inference, explanation, and generalization. Given these difficulties, small wonder that we remain with the tried and true: lecturing, a knowledge in/knowledge out model. Remember that remembering is the lowest level of Bloom's cognitive taxonomy!

In most schools and in most walks of life, knowledge is offered as neat, organized, verified "facts" that can be counted, summarized, condensed, and tested. (For the purposes of our discussion, we will overlook the fact that facts may not always be factual, subject to "checking.")

The age of "Google it" encourages most learners to just pop on over to a handy-dandy computer and collect some "facts." Sources of these facts are frequently overlooked or not even considered (Alverman 2004). Checking is left to experts, specialists, others. Thus, we can be easily duped. This factual knowledge, while valued, is a mile wide and an inch deep, and not very critical. Let's face it, with the aid of the web, students often download their work and present it as a paper well done (Coiro et al. 2008). Sometimes they don't even read it themselves and thus know *less* than nothing.

While students are clear about collecting data, teachers seem very confused about current assignments. Many undertake to cover material while overlooking the many mandates for improving skills, bolstering reasoning, and promoting higher-order thinking. Of course, the educational system itself is conflicted and sends out mixed messages about what is important to learn, "facts" or "skills." Thus, when there is too much pressure, teachers revert to the bottom line of education—scores based on simple factual knowledge.

Into this situation comes the creative teacher who seeks to arouse creative learning, going beyond the facts to reasons, theories, attitudes, and hypotheses. This teacher wants a vibrant classroom of interested, vital students, not sleepers. She or he wants authentic work from a class engaged with its feelings as well as knowledge. However, once these loftier goals are embraced, new needs develop, most particularly the need for greater depth.

Deep knowledge (questions, problems, and issues) drives and sustains creative teaching and learning. Creative ideas flow from depth of knowledge, from a sense of ownership and struggle to work things out alone or with a group of peers. Answers proposed, or insinuated, by a teacher invariably lessen the creative potential of students. In effect, the teacher is supplying missing pieces and conclusions, reducing the students' problem-solving time and skills.

Creative teachers face the difficult task of encouraging and rewarding student-driven thinking, often in a hostile environment. Developing creativity is no mean feat when you are faced with the demands of "coverage" dictated by school curricula and standardized testing,

Teaching creatively is based on research and theories about work and play, how curiosity and initiative are developed, and the nature of knowledge as construction. For a creative teacher, the primary goal is development of insight and thinking skills. Done properly, voyages of discovery across mysterious and turbulent seas reach the shores of a new idea and weigh anchor. How then to proceed as captain of this voyaging vessel?

Students need to progress from lower- to higher-order thinking, feeling, and acting. To accomplish this, a "scaffold" or scale of progress is constructed. We're going to use the latest model of Bloom's taxonomy as a guide (Anderson and Krathwohl 2001), particularly because "creating" is the new top category. This change suits our purposes perfectly!

However, creating and using a scaffold, *any* scaffold, entails some caveats. First, there is the matter of rigidity. Bloom's categories (old and new) should be viewed as *spiral and overlapping* rather than as fixed and totally distinct. Levels feed into each other and walls are permeable as teacher and students glide up (or down) the ladder of thinking, feeling, and acting.

Second, definitions are tricky. It is often difficult to ascertain where, exactly, students are on the continuum. The good news is that even if teachers have only a rough idea of where students are, they will still know whether students are moving upward because higher-order thinking promotes real discussion and student-initiated questions.

Third, the taxonomies are educational objectives, or goals. Creative teachers seek to push, lead, and stimulate learners toward higher-order ideas and applications, but the actual process may be choppy, inconsistent, and a bit chaotic. Students may fall back a notch or two, then jump forward suddenly, seeking reassurance and rest before reaching higher levels. The process is not necessarily linear and should not be forced. Daily discussion and experimentation need not and should not slavishly progress from level one to six; ideas should ebb and flow naturally, even playfully.

Fourth, the levels themselves are less important than what is happening on the ground. If the group is engaged in reasoning, and participants invent their own theories and explanations, they have reached at least middle-order levels. Teachers should know when a student, group, or class is making progress. Precisely defining the level that each and all are at is not particularly fruitful.

Fifth, categories may be used as assessment and diagnostic devices to ascertain students' levels. But the categories and categorizations should always be viewed as open to review and reconsideration. Characterizing or judging a lesson, unit, or course, let alone students and teachers, is a complex matter. This requires discussion and analysis based on as many kinds of data as possible.

Given these caveats, the taxonomy in any version might best be depicted as a spiral of overlapping sets, as shown below:

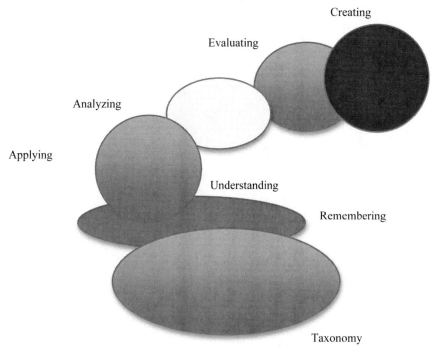

FIGURE 5.1

Creative teaching seeks to move from one level to another, climbing the ladder of thinking, feeling, and acting. And these sets overlap and morph into one another as a lesson, unit, and course evolves. Cutting across these six levels are four knowledge dimensions that also may be used to measure accomplishment.

THE FOUR KNOWLEDGE DIMENSIONS

1. Factual (essential facts basic to specific disciplines);
2. Conceptual (knowledge of definitions, principles, rules, theories for a specific discipline);

3. Procedural (knowledge of methods and skills or investigative techniques applicable to one or more disciplines);
4. Metacognitive (knowledge of cognitive processes, how knowledge is found, used, and applied within and across disciplines, as well as in daily life).

These dimensions of learning offer a means of measuring the process (formative) and outcomes (summative) of creative teaching.

Teachers may begin to excite inquiry by grabbing attention, drawing out ideas, sparking curiosity, stimulating investigations, exploring viewpoints, and provoking judgments. As students progress, they develop questions, problems, and topics that were not supplied by the teacher.

With guidance, students cross into different dimensions, moving from the factual, through the conceptual and procedural, to the metacognitive, thinking about thinking. Students learn to proceed deductively as detectives or inductively as scientists, combining strategies with deep feeling.

THEORY AND PRACTICE IN A CLASSROOM
Uncertain and contested knowledge *stimulates thinking* (Renzulli 1992).

Unsettled and contested answers are open to argument and promote the exchange of ideas. Settled answers don't demand much discussion at all. Uncertainty, ambiguity, and inconsistency can be dear friends to the creative teacher (Sternberg and Lubart 1995). Certainty, by contrast, inhibits creativity because the answers are already known. Students can lean on their teacher, each other, or the textbook. Worse yet, experts have solved problems for them, for us all.

We need only memorize and spit back the "facts," some of which are actually definitions or theories, and perform well on tests. Taking notes on what is already known, or in the text, may be mere repetition, but students have completed the assignment, usually satisfactorily.

From a creative point of view, what have students accomplished? What skills are they demonstrating? Can students explain the data? Have their minds expanded? Faced with new problems, new interpretations, do students know how to proceed? What can teachers do to stimulate creative learning? Teacher-guides can design curricula to facilitate insightful thinking, moving to problem-solving and problem-finding (Sternberg and Williams 1996).

Instructional pathways or strategies fall into six *overlapping instructional categories* that power the engines of creative potential.

SIX "ENGINES" AND QUESTIONS THAT GENERATE CREATIVITY

I) Attention awakened

Attention is awakened when teachers ask about evidence and observation. This includes close and careful scrutiny of the world, contact with raw data, and orientation to environments. Questions call for description and detail (remembering—*not* memorizing!).

II) Ideas aroused

Ideas are aroused when teachers ask about meaning and message: understanding terms; developing categories, definitions, and classifications; drawing analogies and making metaphors. Questions involve meaning and message (understanding).

III) Curiosity sparked

Curiosity is sparked when teachers ask about explanation and hypothesis: applying and analyzing evidence, determining cause and effect, understanding relationships and correlations, making hypotheses and inferences. Questions call for reasons and hypotheses (application through analysis).

IV) Investigations stimulated

Investigations are stimulated when teachers introduce perplexity and mystery: multiple, clashing, and converging views, ambiguity and puzzlement, contradictions and unknowns. Questions involve possibilities and probabilities (analysis through synthesis).

V) Viewpoints explored

Viewpoints are explored when teachers ask about different perspectives and conflicting interpretations: multiple, overlapping, converging, contradictory, and conflicting frames of reference. Questions ask about vantage point and trustworthiness (evaluating through understanding).

VI) Judgments provoked (stirred)

Judgments are provoked when teachers ask about moral issues and material assessments: criteria-based evaluations and moral values, controversies and commitments, debates and decisions, philosophical stands on good and evil. Questions suggest judgments and ethical values (evaluating through understanding and analysis).

Engine I. Awakening Attention

Asking about evidence, description, and detail: From inattention to fascination (close and careful observation)

At the very base of creative thinking is the simple act of close observation (Leschak 1991).

Sherlock Holmes was famous for having a quick eye for detail that allowed him to solve mysteries. Taking in detail is a great talent that we often overlook. Noticing detail is collecting evidence. But evidence (a metaphor for data, information, or facts) can change, grow, and evolve; results are neither settled nor perfect. That is why the word "evidence" is preferable to "facts" in creative teaching.

Evidence forms a basis for drawing conclusions, not necessarily for revealing truth. Truth, or at least its approximation, grows out of evidence. But evidence requires interpretation. The observer must make sense of evidence and test it against other data, reason, and theory (Gardner 1993).

Direct contact with evidence, or detail, is preferable to using textbooks, computer simulations, or scholarly studies that students accept as proven. In teaching, we usually hand students the evidence they need on a silver platter, in no way building their observational skills. In many subjects, such as science, social studies, and art, observation is of the highest importance because specific details are often guides to building or challenging conclusions.

In the real world, many scientists and social scientists have made great discoveries from close observation of phenomena (Csikszentmihalyi 1991). Darwin, for example, developed and tested part of the theory of evolution using specimens of birds, lizards, and butterflies collected on his trip to South America, particularly the Galapagos Islands. Models of the atom and the many particles that compose it are central to observations in physics. Historians and social scientists observe current and past human behavior to formulate theories about causes and consequences. Observations may lead to understanding political decisions, wars, revolutions, economic choices, and so on.

Close observation enhances sensory skills and psychomotor coordination. Focusing on details and recognizing nuances in evidence leads students to compare and formulate conclusions. Results can be tested and retested against new evidence. Using evidence as a base teaches students investigational skills similar to those of a detective. Quick and easy conclusions are questioned rather than readily accepted.

As learners integrate evidence with hypotheses, findings with ideas, conclusions with insight, they begin to appreciate the value of doing their own detective work. They engage the world, viewing it as a place of mystery and discovery, not as grocery lists or data from the electronic "clouds" of the twenty-first century.

So let's draw students into examining facts as evidence. Let's promote close observation of phenomena. Let's give our students "wait-time" sufficient to draw conclusions about evidence. Let's compare ideas with each other and test for truth. Close observation and evidence collection promote careful attention to detail and may awaken the comatose if cleverly presented.

Engine II. Arousing Ideas
Asking about meaning and message: From analogy to eureka! (categories/ definitions, classifications, analogies, similes, and metaphors)

Analogy, definition, and classification are basic powerhouses in teaching creatively.

Naming and labeling, classifying and categorizing are basic elements in organizing thought. They are vital building blocks of thought. Understanding develops as names or definitions are assigned to a wide variety of things, ideas, and actions. This helps us to create a schema for storing and sifting data (Runco 1993). But this schema can also lead to rigidity and narrow-mindedness if one and only one definition, class, or category is viewed as correct.

Definitions, classifications, and categories are concepts. They are NOT data, but tools for labeling sets of data. They may change with time and new discoveries, and as language develops. Many teachers give students definitions as though these are unchallengeable "givens" that can never change. Nothing could be more destructive of creativity because students need to learn how to formulate and test terms. Usage grows out of deeper understanding of words, providing meaning. Application to new cases is essential.

A definition is, in effect, an abstract condensation of a whole class or category of data. Society has codified definitions in dictionaries, which may be very helpful to society but not very useful in creative classrooms. If taught as true, the definition loses its value as a point of discussion and promotes memorization, not critical inquiry. What is a revolution, for instance? Not an easy problem once you dig in. Or what is life? Is a rock alive? Is a virus alive?

Let's struggle against simply accepting one definition as definitive. Let's draw students into the process of developing and testing concepts. Forming their own definitions is a first step toward making sense of disparate data.

Definitions are ideas that pull examples together: analogies. Definitions are built out of data and/or from theory. When we say "hawks," we mean a certain kind of bird. In biology there are classifications of hawks, and hawks are part of a larger family of raptor/ predators, each with somewhat different characteristics. We could even go off on a tangent collecting hawk metaphors, like being a war hawk!

As the number of examples is increased, the overall concept can be tested and refined. Students should rebuild their definitions, concepts, and categories daily, or weekly, during classroom discussion. This enables learners to refine ideas as they are applied to new examples.

Analogies can be drawn from any field of study and may cut across disciplinary lines, for example, revolution from history, shape from mathematics, perspective from art, simile from English or world languages, estimating from math, or evolution from science. As students find likenesses or differences between and among examples, analogies become more focused and criteria better defined.

Similes and metaphors derive from analogies and allow us to make comparisons in "figures of speech." Metaphors create associations between objects and ideas, for example, "imagination is the eye of the soul," according to Joubert, author of *Pensées*. Where metaphors make direct comparisons, similes create indirect links. For example, to paraphrase H. W. Beecher, "imagination is like an observatory without a telescope." Metaphors and similes help us to define ideas in words and images that are richer and more understandable. As students emerge from the box, capabilities for building complex analogies increase geometrically.

Engine III: Sparking Curiosity
Asking about explanations: From higher-order analogy to reasons (causes, correlations, and hypotheses)

A third engine for creative teaching is asking for explanations. Asking why something happened, how something works, or what motives drive action promotes inquiry into correlations, cause and effect. A grasp of cause and effect helps us understand how the world works, guiding and testing the theories.

Again, we want to promote thinking about relationships: *multiple* explanations or *multifactored* analyses, rather identification of the one "right" answer. Students need well-balanced and interesting data to build explanations. Teachers should choose problems that invite hypothesizing about competing solutions.

In real life we revise our ideas all the time, but don't necessarily share them with others. In a creative classroom, we need to learn not just to formulate, but to defend and explain ideas. Teachers can offer competing explanations for students to assess, or ask the learners to critique on their own. In either case, students should explain the reasons for their conclusions. Learners may proceed inductively, using original sources or raw data to reach their conclusions, or they may proceed deductively, evaluating the opinions of "experts" against their evidence.

Inference, a form of explanation, may be viewed as a process of developing interpretations of data. This is a reasoning process that usually begins after observation, puzzlement, and analogizing. Before a teacher or a learner can infer a cause, he or she needs a body of knowledge and practice with reasoning skills. Inference, therefore, grows out of a well-digested database.

As students grapple with evidence or problems they are trying to integrate into a more general rule, they begin to make inferences, for instance, about interest rates, or proportions. Current advertisements from banks offering 1 percent interest in bold letters may seem enticing until they find out that the rate of inflation is 3 percent. The math classroom then becomes both theoretical and practical with a search for proportions, or 1 to 3. This means that putting money in that bank account actually results in a loss of funds when compared to inflation! But then we look for other places to put money and find higher risks, so we are left with a dilemma: where should we put the funds to make money? Or should we simply stash it under our beds?

Data and examples are accumulated, categorized, compared, and contrasted, perhaps quickly, perhaps slowly, and suddenly explanations spring out of students' mouths. Student-initiated explanation is a great victory for a creative teacher because this leads to higher-order thinking. When you turn casually to Johnny or Mary and ask how a combustion engine works, and they can answer in their own words, you are really getting somewhere. If they look flabbergasted, you need to reinvent your lesson. If learners can add a few suggestions for improving the engine, we are in high creative territory. We are out of the box and approaching a wall.

Thus, explanation (reasoning) and its all-inclusive bigger siblings, inference, generalization, and insight, must grow out of evidence and a grasp of concepts. As explanation or insight becomes greater than the sum of its parts, there will be significant advancement to higher-order thinking.

Engine IV: Stimulating Investigations
Asking about perplexity: From puzzlement (mystery) to solution; solving unknowns (puzzles, paradoxes, ambiguities, mysteries, and uncertainties)

A fourth related teaching engine, very powerful, is mystery: the idea of the unknown, the puzzle, the perplexing. Mystery is a favorite art form or genre. We even have a host of metaphors, serious and humorous, to describe the process of mystery: mindbogglers, brain twisters, riddles, stumpers, whodunits, and puzzlers.

Puzzles are composed of pieces, sometimes broken or missing, that must be put together in a meaningful way (Cropley 2005). Missing pieces cause anxiety but also lead to investigation, invention, and theorizing. Puzzles in the larger sense (not the store-bought variety) are a way of getting students' attention and motivating them to find solutions. Solutions need not be complete or final, but should go beyond the "pieces" available to solve the puzzle.

Proposed solutions may guide the search for new clues or the reinterpretation of existing clues. Puzzles can be created at different levels. Data may be available but disorganized, missing, damaged, or distorted. Unknowns have to be filled in, estimated, or interpolated. A really good puzzle involves a sense of mystery, a feeling that the more you find out, the more you need to know.

In an archeological dig, the outcome is not at all a foregone conclusion. Artifacts may or may not lead to full understanding of significance. If there are no symbols or language, the mystery is even greater, but it is a lot more fun to work on by hypothesizing and speculating.

In mathematics, the process of solution, and the use of alternative methods, is pleasurable even after the problem is solved. Solving unknowns is perhaps an analog of detective work in mystery stories. Trying to discover the causes of a disease, Dr. House in action, is also a type of mystery that promotes problem-solving.

We may find evidence of environmental change by studying plants and animals that we ordinarily take for granted. A survey may reveal a decline or extinction of some species. In this kind of scientific investigation, the solution is not fixed and there may be considerable controversy over methods of investigation, as well as results.

Puzzles, therefore, are actually complex tasks and can take many forms (Sternberg and Lubart 1991). All perplex participants because something is missing or ambiguous. Tentative conclusions are interesting (and safer!) because they can be re-examined, like the case for warm-blooded, fast-moving, film-friendly dinosaurs. Puzzlement is exactly what teachers should want in their classrooms: work with uncertain conclusions, ambiguous evidence, contradictory information, paradoxes, and dilemmas.

Unknowns and puzzles are major friends of motivation.

Engine V: Exploring Viewpoints
Asking about perspective: Vantage points (multiple, clashing, and converging) and trustworthiness (believability and corroboration)

Perspective or point of view (POV) is a fifth very powerful engine for teaching creatively, raising questions of alternative interpretations and believability.

The ability to take on multiple perspectives is the beginning of creative maturity (Ifenthaler et al. 2011). A problem or question is examined from different points of view. Learners can stand in others' shoes, outside of themselves. Students and teacher alike go beyond their own views to appreciate others' perspectives. Where once there were one or two views of a problem or issue, there are now multiple versions. Where once there were simple, seemingly factual accounts of events, there are now several, or many, and some of these may compete for primacy.

Multiple perspectives include observations and analogies, interpretations and arguments. Perspectives may be many-sided but not necessarily conflicting. Or they may diverge so sharply that even basic "facts" are in dispute. Even after careful study, there may be a deadlock, a sharp split in views that cannot be reconciled. This panoply of views is at once confusing and interesting.

Perspectives may converge or merge into a complex (and fuller) picture of a person, place, or event, yielding explanations for the variety of perspectives. This "big" picture of a subject is very helpful indeed to comprehension.

Creative teachers can take advantage of multiple or clashing views. We might converge on theories about the warm-bloodedness of dinosaurs, or review the disputes about how to settle the Arab-Israeli or some other intractable conflict, or compare differing perspectives concerning place, a geographic setting, ancient vs. modern, tourist vs. native, rich vs. poor.

Viewpoint/perspective encourages teaching from many angles, for example, insiders and outsiders, protagonists and antagonists, observers and participants. Events can look and feel very different when perspectives come into play. As an example, foreign policy can seem reassuring or upsetting depending on the perspective of the group, side, or nation. Policy can be discussed from a range of theoretical perspectives, not representing any nation in particular, but focusing on humanitarian versus security goals. Perhaps the Martian view will help a true outsider? Each perspective widens the view of an event or policy and leads to an overall position or decision about what may be best or true.

Another example of perspective is how a sample of literary critics may "see" a story in different lights. These views are informed by competing philosophies of literature. The creative instructor might offer a short story and three or four conflicting reviews and then have students write their own.

Viewpoints are springboards for arguments about interpretation, subjectivity, and trustworthiness. Suppose you're planning a vacation. *Fodor's* says Syria is an interesting place, but news reports say the government is shooting its own rebellious citizens. The Syrian government and its opponents have starkly contrasting views. Maybe the visit should be put off a while, or maybe it could be *really* interesting!

Competing or complementary viewpoints promote thinking because most of us are used to having only one take on a topic—what my teacher, or Mom or Dad, or an "expert" told us. Many viewpoints may also be confusing and upsetting because we begin to feel that we can't really find the truth, that perhaps all we have are personal views.

Unfamiliar and unpopular views really can shake up students who are comfortably used to the "one right way." The "other" may disturb our ethnocentric ideas. Students can play roles taken by others, even people seen as enemies, for an introduction to how the "other side" sees "us." Enemy nations, or even friends, can offer quite different perspectives on how to make peace, solve a border dispute, or join for economic benefits.

A skilled diplomat/teacher or student is able to stand in others' shoes and meld demands into agreements. Creative teachers can take advantage of role-play to present many perspectives raising questions about trust and truth, message and meaning.

Engine VI: Judgments Provoked (and Stirred)
Asking about judgments: From apathy to empathy (controversy, debate, commitment, and sympathy)

Provoking judgments, evaluative or emotional, stirs high-level discussions and debates. Judgments are not merely opinions, feelings, or attitudes (Elliott 2007). Rather judgments are requests for reasoned decisions that sum up knowledge and viewpoints. In other words, these are defensible positions, grounded in fact and reason, leading to decisions.

Judgments cross a wide range of topics, issues, and controversies, but always demand criteria, rules, and reasons to support a case. Evaluation, assessment, and taking positions all roughly equate with the process of judging products, human actions, or political and philosophical values.

All forms of judgment express emotions ranging from mild to strong, negative to positive, depending on the context and topic. For the purposes of creative pedagogy, there are two major types of judgment: 1) evaluative/conventional, and 2) moral/ethical.

An evaluative judgment usually involves ranking or choosing a "best" product or process, service or performance. Evaluations can range from "what is the best way to solve a quadratic equation?" to "which car is best?" to the more emotional "can war be just?"

There may be degrees of emotional involvement in choosing a car or deciding on the best method for solving quadratics, but these are basically intellectual/evaluative judgments. Hopefully there is a lot more emotion in a debate about government policy, the death penalty, helping the poor, or just wars, all of them moral issues. Evaluative judgments are usually low in affect, while moral judgments are often warm to hot.

Emotions can vary greatly by issue, with the highest emotional level usually connected to deeply felt moral or ethical choices (Goleman 1998). However, human beings are complex and sometimes relatively innocuous cases may yield hot arguments, such as a government decision to place a homeless shelter or power plant in your neighborhood. Then NIMBY, or "not in my backyard," comes into play. Of course, the hot debate about a shelter or power station is actually about deeply held values concerning "others," the poor, or government interference that affects property values and quality of life.

Creative teachers can take advantage of both evaluative judgment and moral decisions. Judgment is a powerful strategy for promoting creative thinking because it incorporates and connects evidence, ideas, explanations, and perspectives with feelings and values. As soon as an emotional component is added to any conversation, formal or informal, adrenaline helps to sustain inquiry.

Unfortunately, many teachers worry about controversies getting "out of hand" in a classroom, as they do in daily life, and shy away from dealing with judgment. This deprives students of a powerful engine for discussion, rendering many topics inert. For instance, how can the Holocaust be studied without dealing with emotions? How can we discuss a hot presidential election in purely "objective" terms? How can global warming be examined without looking at competing claims and positions, taking a stand on the environment?

Human beings constantly take positions and make judgments about each other, products and services, actions and policies. So why not use this very human characteristic for instructional purposes by *intentionally organizing* for evaluation/valuation through discussion, debate, and role-play? Students enjoy the process of examining issues, particularly if these issues are not too close to bedrock values.

But they also try to avoid taking stands. Indecision, neutrality, and abstaining are fine as long as students participate in the process of judging. There is no need to "rush to judgment" in a classroom, particularly a creative one. In fact, admitting to indecision and confusion is a sign of growth (Hoffman 2000). Nonetheless, teachers should push toward making a decision or endorsing a position, teaching how to consider and channel feelings into reasons.

Decisions require reflection and re-examination of the evidence and arguments on all sides. This takes time and thought, and should not be rushed. Quick choices forced by leaders or teachers probably do not reflect commitment. Philosophies require testing and time to evolve before a position grows that really reflects and defines a person, group, classroom, or community. Thus, teachers should return to and review decisions throughout the year.

Most students will eventually arrive at a degree of understanding and commitment, judgment that will surprise everyone.

THE SPECIAL CASE OF CONTROVERSY

Judgment-making may be applied to any subject: art, science, or mathematics, but usually involves evaluation rather than controversy. Controversy is a special, and highly motivating, subset of judging, and it requires skillful organization, a balancing act between "light" and "heat," reason and emotions. Controversy develops when competing and conflicting perspectives emerge on an issue. Teachers can encourage student debate by raising policy questions and by offering unpopular or unfamiliar stands on controversial topics. The students may offer a variety of clashing views and emotions that spark arguments.

Emotions and feelings fuel sharing of arguments and positions, building on previous inquiry, and raise the conversation to a new level of commitment (Thoma 1994). Students begin to formulate positions, taking sides and rethinking values, developing a sense of their own views and whether they should act upon them. Controversy or "sidedness" builds argumentative skills. Students are no longer comparing and evaluating differing viewpoints.

They are taking and defending a specific position. Debating issues or arguing interpretations implies that we are ready to take sides (and there may be many more than two), to stand up for a principle or standard. This is not a casual expression of opinion anymore, but the formation of a belief. In effect, this is the beginning of a philosophy of life. Will we identify ourselves as liberals or conservatives, hawks or doves, pessimists or optimists? Is it war or peace? Shall we choose apathy, empathy, or sympathy? Must we take a position at all?

Not having a position or stand is close to apathy, although that is a rather unkind word. Perhaps we might call this stand "neutral" or "undecided." We are not going to take a position, but for good reasons. We want to abstain to think a bit more, or we simply dislike the available choices and seek to find a better one. If we select empathy, then we have moved to a position of being open to a judgment, trying out a new feeling.

Creative teachers seek to instill qualities of empathy, keeping options open for re-examination and reconsideration. New evidence may change views; better reasons may be offered, or new perspectives may arise. Fruitful discussion and debate grow from the rich soil of empathy, a willingness to consider different sides. Without it, students' positions may harden and they may stop listening to differing viewpoints.

As creative teachers, we hope that positions, once formed and defended, are not so hardened they are immune to change. A well-developed position should allow alterations in the light of new evidence, new arguments, new times, and new problems.

A delicate problem in the art of creative teaching is pushing for commitment while tolerating and trying to understand other positions.

THE ROLE OF EMOTION IN CREATIVE TEACHING AND LEARNING

At the highest philosophical level, taking a stand encompasses a reasonable balance of emotion and knowledge.

Emotions underlie all learning, for those in the role of students and for teachers, too (Kögler 2000). The subjects we love, the interests we develop, and the activities we enjoy grow out of affection. School can be a terrible place if we have no affection for any subjects or for any teachers. Yet schools also tend to do relatively little to foster or channel student emotions in constructive directions. Subjects are often presented as "factual" curricula that teachers discuss in dispassionate ways and students learn objectively and efficiently.

All of us have talents and interests. We feel affection for some topics and loathing for others, unsure of the reasons behind our choices. Much of this derives from childhood encouragement or lack thereof. Even more derives from school experiences with teachers who were warm and supportive or dull, distant, and harsh. Emotional reactions shape our attitudes toward teaching and learning, and may work toward our growth and success or block our enjoyment and understanding.

One of the critical values of teaching creatively is a harmonious joining of knowledge, thought, feelings, and action. We recognize the role of emotions in learning and promote affection for a subject by engaging learners in engaging activities. We draw learners in with mysterious puzzles, competing viewpoints, surprising insights, and heated debate, employing emotions to fuel the engines of learning. Whether aware of it or not, we seek a rush of adrenaline from the students and from ourselves.

Emotions can cut across all six engines, across any subject, and within a particular conversation or lesson. Judgments are perhaps the most sharply defined expressions of emotion, the most controlled, because solid arguments require facts and reasons. Evidence and explanation must support eventual choices, thereby restraining emotions from running wild as some fear they will.

Emotions are more likely to go out of control at lower levels of cognition when students' opinions are largely unexamined. Many people do not understand their own feelings and make choices, reacting viscerally, expressing views in a crude or violent manner. Strong opinions, often without consideration, erupt based on familial, social, or cultural identifications that are learned but not examined. In such a context more heat than light might be shed on a subject. But this makes the creative teacher's role of empathic guide and questioner all the more valuable. A creative teacher will use emotions to drive learning and will on occasion *carefully* express emotions in public, inviting others to do likewise.

QUESTIONS ACROSS THE SIX ENGINES: A METACOGNITIVE SWEEP!

Questions across the six engines are a crucial weapon in the teacher's arsenal to promote creative thinking. However, questions come in many sizes, varieties, and levels. What questions are posed, in which sequence, and how they affect learners are based on the evidence available, the social context, and the teacher's personal philosophy, educational theory, psychological assumptions, and perception of students' capabilities.

Asking powerful and stimulating questions is a key to teaching creatively, but not an easy skill to acquire. Most teachers see themselves as conveyors of information and therefore basically lecture. They tell what they know to their audience, which may or may not be interested, which may or may not be capable of absorbing the data.

As guides to creative teaching, questions can be categorized into lower-, middle-, and higher-order levels, using a variety of definitions. The definitions matter less than the actual process that drives teaching. If a teacher, consciously or unconsciously, has a grasp of the order of questions and their relative difficulty, then a lesson will significantly enhance student thinking.

Teachers who progressively raise levels of questioning increase their chances for building a creative classroom. Moving upward across the six engines of growth, whether in an orderly or erratic manner, promotes creative insight and an attitude of engagement. This process of scaffolding can cycle and recycle many times, but movement is generally toward higher-level thinking. If a teacher follows a didactic, recitation type of questioning, then the results will remain on a relatively low level.

Questions and answers are key indicators of the direction in which teaching and learning are headed in any classroom. A great deal of give and take among and between students and teacher(s) is a sign of engagement, a characteristic of creative teaching. Conversely, if questions and answers are brief, and mostly teacher to student, student to teacher, thinking is at a relatively low level.

The goals of questioning really matter. A teacher headed toward a specific answer, a right answer, will find it very difficult to break out of this pattern and promote independent thinking, much less creativity. Another teacher headed toward fostering alternative answers (and questions) will yield quite a different classroom atmosphere, with a lot of ideas flowing. The students will experience a feeling of intellectual and moral growth. Participation will rise and spread within the group.

Questions, especially provocative questions of a higher order, provide the spark plugs for the six engines of creative teaching.

SUMMARY AND CONCLUSIONS

We began by comparing traditional methods of teaching with the higher-order goals posited in Bloom's taxonomy and others. To reach these higher levels, six "engines" for growth in creative teaching and learning were presented.

The goal of the entire enterprise is the production not merely of "knowledge," but of understanding, insight, activity, and feelings. Discoveries, definitions, explanations, solutions, viewpoints, and issues count most when coming from the learner. The teacher's role lies in a skilled arranging of data, designing lessons, providing course architecture, and asking powerful questions.

Those in the teacher role learn how to create a classroom atmosphere that puts students at ease, allowing them to explore and discuss ideas, consider and debate points of view. As learning progresses, students take the initiative, working with raw data to develop theories and explanations at increasingly higher levels, also developing, evaluating, and debating judgments. For the teacher, designing lessons, units, and courses takes on new meaning as evidence is restructured to bolster motivation and improve skills.

Above all, teachers must have sympathy for the bewildered and befuddled learner (signs of real engagement) combined with an experimental view of the classroom. Reflect upon and follow a few key rules for creatively adapting the six engines to your classroom:

- Diagnostics rather than assessments should rule the day.
- Keep creative minds open to observation, perspectives, and feelings.
- Choose and save those lessons, techniques, and questions that arouse and stimulate thinking.
- Keep a firm commitment to multiple outcomes, to the potential for many answers.
- Ask provocative questions without the need to tie everything together into a neat little package that explains the meaning of life.

Creative teachers need to rethink their roles, seeing themselves as guide, provocateur, and questioner rather than director and producer. Acting as a guide is dramatically different from traditional, settled notions of teaching, and it powerfully and purposefully brings instruction to life.

Creative teaching works to enhance our own mental health along with the students'. Recent research indicates that the following characteristics flow from creative teaching:

1. Low inhibition and anxiety
2. Capacity to structure problems in a larger context
3. High fluency and flexibility of ideation
4. High capacity for visual imagery and fantasy
5. High ability to concentrate
6. High empathy with external processes and objects
7. High empathy with people
8. Accessibility of unconscious resources
9. Ability to associate seemingly dissimilar elements in meaningful ways
10. High motivation
11. Capacity to visualize the completed solution in its entirety

---

TEXTBOX 5.1

OUT OF THE BOX

What is your view of the engines of teaching, creative or not?

What do you see as the most stimulating and successful instructional methods? The least?

How would you add, subtract, or change the questions that drive higher order thinking, feeling, and acting?

How would you design a classroom and use technology to stimulate creativity?

REFERENCES

Alverman, D. E., ed. 2004. *Adolescents and Literacies in a Digital World.* New York: Peter Lang.

Amabile, T. 1983. *The Social Psychology of Creativity.* New York: Springer-Verlag.

Anderson, L. W., and D. R. Krathwohl, eds. 2001. *A Taxonomy for Learning, Teaching, and Assessing: A Revision of Bloom's Taxonomy of Educational Objectives.* Complete edition. New York: Longman.

Baddeley, A. 2002. *Human Memory: Theory and Practice,* revised edition. New London, CT: Psychology Press (Taylor and Francis).

Byrnes, J. P. 2001. *Cognitive Development and Learning in Instructional Contexts.* 2nd ed. Boston: Allyn and Bacon.

Coiro, J., M. Knobel, C. Lankshear, and D. J. Leu. 2008. "Central Issues in New Literacies and New Literacies Research." In *The Handbook of Research in New Literacies,* edited by Coiro, Knobel, Lankshear, and Leu. Mahwah, NJ: Erlbaum Publishers.

Cropley, A. J. 2001, 2005. *Creativity in Education and Learning: A Guide for Teachers and Educators.* New York: Routledge/Falmer.

Csikszentmihalyi, M. 1988. *Society, Culture, and Person: A Systems View of Creativity.* In *The Nature of Creativity,* edited by R. J. Sternberg. New York: Cambridge University Press.

Elliott, D. 2007. *Ethics in the First Person: A Guide to Teaching and Learning Practical Ethics.* Lanham, MD: Rowman and Littlefield.

Gardner, H. 1993. *Creating Minds.* New York: Basic Books.

Goleman, D. 1998. *Working with Emotional Intelligence.* New York: Bantam Books.

Hoffman, M. L. 2000. *Empathy and Moral Development.* Cambridge: Cambridge University Press.

Ifenthaler, D., P. Isaias, M. Spector-Kinshuk, et al., eds. 2011. *Multiple Perspectives on Problem Solving and Learning in the Digital Age.* New York and Dordrecht: Springer Verlag.

Kögler, H.H. 2000. "Empathy, Dialogical Self, and Reflexive Interpretation." In *Empathy and Agency: The Problem of Understanding in the Human Sciences,* edited by H. H. Kögler and K. Stueber, 194–206. Boulder, CO: Westview Press.

Leschak, P. 1991. "The Five-Step Creativity Workout." *Writer's Digest* 70 (11): 4–29.

Renzulli, J. 1992. "A General Theory for the Development of Creative Productivity through the Pursuit of Ideal Acts of Learning." *Gifted Child Quarterly* 36 (4): 170–82.

Runco, M. 1993. "Divergent Thinking, Creativity, and Giftedness." *Gifted Child Quarterly* 37 (1): 16–22.

Schacter, Daniel L. 2001. *The Seven Sins of Memory: How the Mind Forgets and Remembers.* Boston: Houghton Mifflin.

Sternberg, R. J. 1997. *Successful Intelligence.* New York: Plume.

Sternberg, R., and T. Lubart. 1991. "Creating Creative Minds." *Phi Delta Kappan* 72 (8): 608–14.

———. 1995. *Defying the Crowd: Cultivating Creativity in a Culture of Conformity.* New York: Free Press.

Sternberg, R. J., and W. M. Williams. 1996. *How to Develop Student Creativity.* Alexandria, VA: Association for Supervision and Curriculum Development.

Thoma, S. 1994. "Moral Judgments and Moral Action." In *Moral Development in the Professions: Psychology and Applied Ethics,* edited by J. R. Rest and D. Narvaez, 199–212. Hillsdale, NJ: Lawrence Erlbaum.

Part II

ENGINES OF CREATIVITY

The second part of creative teaching concerns ways of implementing playful, creative lesson planning at each stage of thinking and across a variety of subjects.

These chapters are offered to stimulate thinking about curriculum design and presentation. Feel free to create a lesson for the level and subject you teach, or for your job or business, or home entertainment. Dissension and controversy are welcome antidotes to all claims made, and valued supplements to any views that have been expressed. Conflict and disagreement can be very creative (Johnson and Johnson 2007).

The five chapters that follow move from the lower to the higher stages of the cognitive, affective, and psychomotor taxonomies as follows:

Chapter 6: Attention awakened (close scrutiny/observation)

Chapter 7: Ideas aroused (definition/analogy/analysis)

Chapter 8: Investigations stimulated (deduction/induction/mystery)

Chapter 9: Viewpoints explored (perspective/complementary and clashing)

Chapter 10: Judgments provoked (evaluation and moral judgment)

An eleventh, and final, chapter provides a wrap-up and discussion of what teaching and learning could be like if education escaped its nineteenth-century industrial roots and entered the twenty-first and twenty-second centuries. This is the "Digi-glob" Age, or Digital Global Age of Great Knowledge (mostly stored) and Great Distraction (mostly whatever is current).

Before examining the examples in each section of part II, you might consider the principles of creativity offered by a noted researcher who claims we all need "a whack on the side of the head" to get going (Van Oech 1983).

1. Generate as many answers as possible. Don't look for the one "right answer."
2. Don't ask if something is "logical."
3. Set aside all rules.
4. Don't judge the quality of an idea by looking at its "practicality."
5. Allow ambiguity.
6. Don't worry about being wrong.
7. Indulge yourself . . . let yourself play.
8. Let yourself go into new areas.
9. Be foolish and silly.
10. Accept your own creativity.
11. Make yourself receptive to new ideas.

Do you agree with any or all of the eleven principles?

Could you actually put more than three into effect in your own teaching and learning?

Are there any you would add, or subtract, or change? Why?

REFERENCES

Johnson, D., and R. Johnson. 2007. *Creative Controversy: Intellectual Challenges in the Classroom.* Edina, MN: Interaction Book Co.

Van Oech, R. 1983. *A Whack on the Side of the Head.* New York: Warner Books.

6

Attention Awakened

The Power of Observation and Participation

"Learning is the discovery that something is possible."

—Fritz Perls

"Men have sought to make a world from their own conception and to draw from their own minds all the material which they employed, but if, instead of doing so, they had consulted experience and observation, they would have the facts and not opinions to reason about, and might have ultimately arrived at the knowledge of the laws which govern the material world."

—Sir Francis Bacon, *Novum Organum Scientarium*, London, 1650

INTRODUCTION

Creative teachers awaken attention by appealing to students' senses to observe detail, treating evidence as gold.

Contact with the "raw materials" of a subject invites attention. This is coupled with an exploration of settings and examination of samples. Building interest is a basic lower-order strategy that helps learners pay attention to detail for problem-finding (McCrae 1987).

Expert testimony and textbooks can be employed after students have learned how to look, listen, and "feel" using all their senses. The primary

Description

Drama   Discovery

FIGURE 6.1

appeal is to the psychomotor and cognitive domains. Questions about description and detail (remembering and comprehending) are foundations for awakening attention (Schank 1988).

AWAKENING THE STUDENTS

To begin at the beginning, a creative teacher must awaken the students. Unfortunately, bright and excited students are not easy to come by or to manufacture. Lighting the bulb takes considerable technique and starts with evoking human curiosity.

Curiosity, drama, and a sense of mystery are deep drivers of discovery, creating propulsion toward acquiring knowledge (Sternberg 2007). That is why play is so important in human and adult development. Noticing elements of the natural world, watching behavior, piecing information together, and playing with ideas are bases for creative thinking. Only after an awakening can evidence be collected and analyzed.

First we have to be conscious of our surroundings.

Next comes attention, and then discovery follows observation, accompanied by the excitement of participation.

3 LESSON PLANS: IN THE BOX, OUT OF THE BOX, AND OFF THE WALLS

Interest in the environment requires attention and the beginnings of data acquisition. So let's look at a pair of limbs (are they hands or feet?) and predict what kind of creature belongs to these. As a first step, we'll draw the rest of the creature, estimating its size and deciding what sort of setting it is most likely to live in.

We'll look at more hands and feet later on for comparison and think about the purpose of hands and feet; why do some creatures have three toes while others sport five? Fascinated, are you, or inattentive? Why? Perhaps we can review three lessons on this subject and decide what characterizes "in the box," "out of the box," and "off the walls."

Lessons can be direct and literal, in the box, examining what is given and tightly directed by the teacher. Or they can emerge from the box and ask unusual questions, drawing analogies to other ecological systems, calling for comparisons to our own bodies and characteristics. Finally, lessons can be expanded well beyond the box or its neighborhood to include questions that elicit broader comparisons to other ecological systems and call upon learners to extrapolate knowledge and predict what kinds of lifeforms would exist in the same setting. In short, each level of lesson expands the field of inquiry, builds new analogies or metaphors, and eventually asks for creative invention by the participants, both speculative and evidence-based.

In-the-Box Lesson

The aye-aye (*Daubentonia madagascariensis*) is a lemur, a primate native to Madagascar that combines rodent-like teeth and a special thin middle finger to fill the same ecological niche as a woodpecker. It is the world's largest nocturnal primate, and is characterized by its unusual method of

FIGURE 6.2
An aye-aye looking for a snack. Drawing by Joseph Wolf (1820–
1899). A copy in the Richard Own Drawings Collection, Natural
History Museum of London. Original source: "On the Aye-aye,"
Transactions of the Zoological Society 5 (1): 33–101.

finding food; it taps on trees to find grubs, then gnaws holes in the wood
and inserts its narrow middle finger to pull the grubs out. The only other
animal species known to find food in this way is the striped possum. From
an ecological point of view the aye-aye fills the niche of a woodpecker, as it
is capable of penetrating wood to extract the invertebrates within. (Adapted
from Piper 2007.)

Questions:

1. What is an aye-aye?
2. Where does the aye-aye live?
3. How does it find food?

4. What special physical abilities does it have?
5. What family of animals is it related to?
6. Why is it compared to a woodpecker?
7. What are invertebrates?

Out-of-the-Box Lesson

The aye-aye is a mammal from Madagascar, a member of the primate family called lemurs that live in the rain forest of that large island. They are about the size of a squirrel but have some unusual physical features, especially eyes and hands. Take a look at the picture of the aye-aye and think about what purpose the large eyes might serve. Then think about the purpose of the unusually long fingers, especially the middle finger.

Questions:

1. What kind of animal is an aye-aye?
2. What family of animals does it belong to?
3. Why might an animal living in a forest have such long fingers and why such a long middle one?
4. What might this animal like to eat? Does it eat plants, fruit and nuts, or insects? How do you know?
5. Would it move about during the day or at night? How do you know?
6. Is the aye-aye like us or different, or both or neither? How and why?
7. Would you like an aye-aye in your house as a pet? Why or why not?

Off-the-Walls Lesson

Take a look at this drawing of a rather unusual animal called an aye-aye. It is a small mammal that lives on the large island of Madagascar, near the equator off the coast of Africa. It lives in a kind of rain forest environment. Carefully inspect its body and look at what it is holding in the picture.

Questions:

1. Is it a kitty with long fingernails? A fake? Is it a squirrel that looks like a monkey?
2. What features do you notice, for example, hands, face, eyes, body, and so on? Where is the animal? What sort of environment does it probably inhabit? Why?

3. How many fingers does it have and why are they so long? Why is one very long? Do the big eyes tell you anything about its habits?

4. What does the aye-aye probably eat? Is it likely to be a vegetarian or a meat-eater? Does it eat plants or insects or other animals? How can you decide?

5. Does it look like any other animals you might know? Are the hands like ours? Is it related to humans in any way, apes? How can you tell?

6. To be really sure about the aye-aye and its habitat, what research would you need to do? Explain. Are you happy with a drawing as a source? Would you like to have a photo, too? Would photos or drawings be better evidence? Why or why not?

7. What kind of new evidence would help? A video of the animal's behavior? Photographs? A personal interview?

8. Could you design an animal or insect or tree that would live well in the aye-aye's home environment?

A SENSE OF DISCOVERY

In the hands of a creative teacher, a sense of discovery is encouraged, praised, and guided. Examining data and seeking evidence is a powerful basic engine for growth. Go out of your way to arrange lessons that provide for observation, discovery, and insight. This is usually accomplished by presenting attention-getting evidence within an open-ended curriculum design (Feldman 1999). Discovery evolves from provocative lesson planning and careful attention to questioning.

Evidence (the material presented) is set up to draw attention and sustain inquiry. The burden of play and work is placed on students. The teacher's role is proposing questions and guiding discussion, not giving conclusions. In this first step toward creative teaching there is a huge difference between "learning by discovery" and "acquiring knowledge." There are three main differences between the two.

In learning by discovery, students: 1) make direct contact with the content, 2) actively interpret the evidence, and 3) develop positive attitudes of interest, empathy, and value judgment.

If an individual or group of students doesn't connect, is passive, or rejects the content, teaching will be difficult. Willing students are always preferable to an apathetic group. Excited students who are attentive and active are the foundation for self-initiated learning. Students are *key partners* in creative teaching.

In the **first stage,** discovery teaching encourages paying attention by allowing learners to directly experience content, providing provocative questions to guide and inspire their thinking (Bruner 1960). It is crucial that learners begin to use their senses to notice phenomena "in the raw." They begin to see, feel, touch, sense, and regard content as problematical, promoting questions, evoking mysteries. Questions flow from and with the evidence.

Direct contact with primary sources yields results that can range from descriptive lists to higher-order insights. The point is that it is the learner doing this, not the teacher, not an expert in the field, not the textbook. Observational skills start with an item or a reading; students identify details and use them to determine significance or gain understanding.

Once some observations have been made, teachers can begin to encourage understanding and interpretation. Understanding is vital to the process because that is a stage of higher thinking in which the learner tries to define and explain a phenomenon. Observations are integrated, tied to definitions, and ready to use in building analogies.

The **second stage** involves much more than observation. Based on their observations, students begin to reach tentative conclusions that are open to revision and criticism. Teachers and students begin to analyze and apply knowledge, testing definitions and clarifying concepts. Curiosity comes into play as competing explanations are considered and alternative ideas are applied to new and existing data.

At this point, students may want more data or a second or third look at information they already have. When this happens, teachers should jump for joy. This signals a sense of fascination with an inquiry and a commitment to work on a solution. The students are alive with interest. The ball is heading toward the goalpost. The teacher should not tackle the runners.

The **third stage** reinforces interest. Material can be enriched with new information that may provide some answers, but also raises new questions and problems. The process of inquiry can itself become an object of instruction as learners create operational rules to guide their research (Isen, Daubman, and Nowicki 1987). This is the stage when students *know how to ask for additional evidence to understand the aye-aye.*

These operational rules allow students to distinguish reality from fabrication, test truth claims, and rank levels of reasoning. In effect, the original observations and midpoint interpretations are recycled, revised, and refined. Students are now ready to compare their ideas with those of experts.

Scholarly and expert conclusions are, of course, necessary to acquiring an education, but must be handled in a way that does not undermine or replace learning. If scholarly, expert, or textbook knowledge comes too early in the process of discovery, or if teachers endorse answers as true, then the inquiry is undone. How can students, new learners, intelligently grasp the refined knowledge of experts if they have no contact with the raw materials, the original evidence? How can they understand scholars' views if they have no views of their own for comparison?

One of the great flaws of teachers is their need to provide students with "correct" answers. This leads to a host of issues about who is producing the knowledge and who is consuming it. Students may well memorize a "correct" answer, but it may not make sense to them. They will be uninterested and uninvolved.

Would you like an assignment to memorize the telephone book? Would you like a teacher who begins by demanding that you memorize the periodic table, the dynasties of ancient Egypt, the past tense of every verb in German? These assignments treat knowledge as established fact rather than evidence. They may also be a formula for apathy, resistance, and confusion.

The whole point of close scrutiny and careful observation is that creative teachers arrange and assist student contact with the subject matter. Having

TEXTBOX 6.1

CREATIVE EXPERIMENT

How much of a list can your students retain, and for how long? Can students explain what the list is used for? What is included? Why? Why the information is arranged as it is? Choose a list that's relevant to your subject. If students cannot define terms or explain answers, they do not have a real grasp of the information.

a wide range of interests keeps the mind and body young and curious, and healthier. At any age, we can experience the joys of close scrutiny of evidence. Minds open to new discoveries, later bolstered by scholarship and expertise. Neurons and brain cells awaken and expand to accommodate new information as hypotheses are compared with expert opinion.

So let's learn (and teach) the process of close scrutiny of evidence all over again!

HANDS-ON ACTION

Especially because we live in an age of electronics and easy access to data, we remain mindful of the advantages of direct contact with materials. That is not to say that the computer isn't a wonderful invention and that having all that information available at the touch of a finger isn't marvelous. It is! However, teachers need to provide hands-on activities that encourage use of the senses. This means using one or more of our five senses and our sixth sense, the social/emotional, to promote experience and sustain inquiry. The senses deliver direct messages about any subject that a flat computer screen, though highly sophisticated, cannot provide.

There is value in being able to see and handle an industrial object up close. Constructing a mathematical model produces a level of understanding that the two-dimensional model may not deliver. Going to a pond and collecting a cup of organisms to look at under a microscope beats a directed online view. Sticking your nose into a large flower to smell it and feel its texture gives a bee's view and a nose sense not available from a photo, at least right now.

Networking face to face to decide if President Truman was right in ordering the A-bomb dropped on Hiroshima and Nagasaki is better than an online chat for reading body language and facial expressions. Face-to-face, hands-on encounters afford a raw three-dimensional view of learning, one not pre-packaged for consumption. Maybe a final decision hangs fire, but you have a more tuned-in feeling for everyone's views.

Schools, being what they are, tend to offer far too much in the way of pre-packaged experiences. These include texts, worksheets, prepared lesson plans, and media that orient and solidify a learner's grasp of a topic. In many cases, this experience can be over-directed as the designer leads students through a pre-arranged sequence to a specific conclusion. The whole lesson belongs out there to someone else.

In contrast, close scrutiny (observation) needs to be planned in ways that awaken the senses of slumbering students. Evidence is designed to foster hands-on contact and interpretation. In many disciplines, hands-on learning can be accomplished quite simply by bringing in objects, conducting experiments, building models, and playing games. Some topics are easier to relate to directly than others, but there are always ways to provide sensory input.

For example, mathematics, perhaps one of the most abstract subjects in the curriculum, can easily be presented in hands-on fashion. Teachers can provide straws or sticks with which to build geometric models or do fractions with real objects. How about cutting a ruler in half, or quartering or "eighting" a pizza pie and then eating it as a reward?

Science is easy to turn into direct contact, and, surprisingly, so is social studies. Instead of talking about industrialization, why not look at a set of "mystery" objects from the nineteenth and twentieth centuries and attempt to identify their functions? Combine science with history to promote investigation of industry from different angles.

Organize inquiry around a prominent human sixth sense, the social/emotional. The social sense makes use of students working in pairs, groups, or teams. Although social networking comes quite easily, among students it is usually focused on personal matters. However, groups can be organized to promote learning with significant advantages (and disadvantages) over individual study.

Working in groups, from pairs on up, promotes sharing ideas and decision-making. A basically democratic structure usually gives students in a group access to the same material and a share in developing and negotiating conclusions. Groups are ideal for discussing observations and making moral decisions. Issues can be raised about who to vote for, what makes a great story, and which policies have good outcomes.

Forming groups can be difficult. Students want to stay with their friends and may argue about group assignments. In heterogeneous groupings of students with varying abilities, better students may overwhelm the weaker ones, or the weaker ones could lazily follow along or sabotage a lesson. Perhaps teams of two pairs would be better for research than larger groups, particularly if teachers cannily match students by interests and skills.

Students in larger groups may have varying assignments. One might read a document aloud, while another records varying interpretations. One or two others could be assigned the task of verifying and cross-checking disputed or contradictory information. Individuals or perhaps pairs might cover material more quickly but in less depth.

Finally, hands-on contact can also make use of our "seventh" sense: insight, intuition, and imagination. Teachers take advantage of the materials available and ask students to produce something imaginative, individually or in groups. Productions might range from role-plays and ad hoc scripts, through new twists on experiments, to artistic endeavors.

Learners extend, adapt, shape, and revise the materials under discussion to produce a new version (really new or new to them) of a topic. Teachers hope that students will go beyond the data given to create a version that shows enrichment and extension. Moving from initial hands-on through group activity to higher-order levels of imaginative work sustains and increases self-confidence. Learners gather strength and skill in improvisation and interpretation from a solid base of observation.

Of course, not all students will immediately be able to grasp ideas or extend what they have learned into imaginative products. But a consistent pattern of direct contact and productivity will allow this to become a legitimate everyday goal. Thus, close scrutiny of evidence slowly but surely increases potential for imagination and insight, leading (eventually) to student-directed discovery and invention.

DISCOVERY

Discovery is the stage at which students interpret the evidence for themselves. In effect, they "discover" new ideas, principles, and conclusions. Bruner, a noted psychologist, is credited with coining the term "discovery learning" to describe this awakening of interest (Bruner 1960).

The term "discovery" was popular in the 1960s and '70s when the United States was competing with the Soviet Union for world dominance. Part of this competition centered on education. Many creative projects in the sciences, mathematics, social sciences, history, and the humanities were funded based on a philosophy of inquiry derived from the pragmatism of John Dewey (Dewey 1916). Curriculum units were deliberately hands-on, combining evidence with theory to promote discovery and test basic principles within and across subjects.

The argument for "discovery" is that detailed examination of evidence leads to insights (Bruner 1967). Discovery as a process is akin to a skilled detective

noticing clues, however insignificant, and building inferences. Hands-on encounters with the materials work to strengthen and test first impressions. Ideas
are shared, collated, and interpreted to explain the findings. Insights follow with
improved process skills in each field. Students learn *a process* of investigation
along with the *content* of a subject. They acquire tools for interpretation that
may be applied to new evidence. Interpretations may be achieved slowly and
painstakingly, or by sudden insight into underlying principles.

The concept of discovery implies that new territory has been traversed,
at least for the learner (Holland et al. 1986). However, as Columbus did not
discover the New World, students do not often venture into totally uncharted
landscapes. Curricula are arranged so that students think about many avenues for making sense of the materials presented.

Raising levels of interest and imagination is precisely the point of discovery.
Learners who have really done their homework with evidence, worked hands-
on, and considered ideas may suddenly express an "aha!" or "eureka!" This
flash of discovery is vitally important to creativity at all levels because it signals
a breakthrough, an awakening of interest, deeper attention to a problem.

For example, an understanding of the solar system once consisted of being
able to name the planets. This has evolved into discovery of an astronomical
system governed by a gravitational, rotating, variable set of forces. Separate
celestial bodies are placed in a larger context—solar system, galaxy, and uni-
verse—with new possibilities to explore.

At this point, if student fascination grows, teachers can become a lot more
serious about teaching astronomy. They have students' attention! Learners
are beginning to put evidence together using big ideas. Teachers no longer
have to spoonfeed data and train memory to reinforce learning. Students seek
more questions and answers on their own without extrinsic rewards.

CONCLUSION: RAISING QUESTIONS ABOUT AWAKENING ATTENTION

As observations expand, students seek out knowledge on their own. They
may consult online sources, go to a museum or planetarium, read a book,
or construct their own project that ties into the topic. More importantly,
they begin to ask questions, lots of questions, moving to higher-order, more
thought-provoking questions. Questions begin to drive the inquiry.

And questions are keys to growth, development, and the refinement of
ideas. Close scrutiny at first yields low-level questions and some answers.

BONUS BOX LESSON

Have you ever discovered a triangle?

What is a triangle? Can you invent its formula? Are all triangles equal?

Does a triangle have any uses, past or present?

Can you discover triangles in daily life, right now?

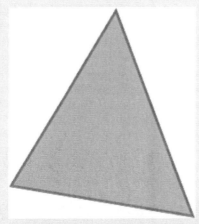

FIGURE 6.3A

FIGURE 6.3B

(continued)

BONUS BOX LESSON (*continued*)

How would you design a building that would last: would it be a triangle, rectangle, or square? Why?

Which would be strongest?

Which would get the most attention?

Which is the loveliest design?

What forms are you attracted to? Have you thought about it?

A bit later, hands-on experience yields increasingly higher-level interpretations. Students are ready to have their curiosity sparked and investigations stimulated. Motivation to press onward and upward has been brought to life by the discovery process. Now it needs to be sustained through increasingly challenging questions.

Ideas begin to flow and interpretations multiply. Questions lead to more questions and the learning enterprise begins to take on a life of its own.

REFERENCES

Bruner, J. 1960. *The Process of Education.* Cambridge, MA: Harvard University Press.

———. 1967. *On Knowing: Essays for the Left Hand.* Cambridge, MA: Harvard University Press.

Dewey, J. 1916. *Democracy and Education.* New York: Free Press.

Feldman, D. H. 1999. "The Development of Creativity." In *Handbook of Creativity,* edited by R. J. Sternberg. Cambridge, UK: Cambridge University Press.

Holland, J. H., K. J. Holyoak, R. E. Nisbett, and P. Thagard. 1986. *Induction: Processes of Inference, Learning, and Discovery.* Cambridge, MA: MIT Press.

Isen, A. M., K. A. Daubman, and G. P. Nowicki. 1987. "Positive Affect Facilitates Creative Problem Solving." *Journal of Personality and Social Psychology* 52:1122–31.

McCrae, R. R. 1987. "Creativity, Divergent Thinking, and Openness to Experience." *Journal of Personality and Social Psychology* 52 (6): 1258–65.

Piper, R. 2007. *Extraordinary Animals: An Encyclopedia of Curious and Unusual Animals.* Westport, CT: Greenwood Press.

Schank, R. C. 1988. *The Creative Attitude: Learning to Ask and Answer the Right Questions.* New York: Macmillan.

Sternberg, R. J. 2007. *Wisdom, Intelligence, and Creativity Synthesized.* New York: Cambridge University Press.

Ideas Aroused

Formulating Definitions and Building Analogies

"It don't mean a thing, if it ain't got that swing."

—Duke Ellington

"What happens to the hole when the cheese is gone?"

—Bertolt Brecht

INTRODUCTION

Forming ideas is the middle ground of thinking and feeling, an often slow but necessary step toward higher ground.

Creative teachers *ask about meaning, message, and metaphor* so students will solidify ideas. Developing categories and classifications, drawing analogies, and creating metaphors are key aids in the reasoning process. Reasoning processes, therefore, form the midlevel building blocks that support growth toward higher levels of skill, thinking, and attitudinal development.

Definitions and metaphors, analogies and classifications draw upon previous observations but go a step or two further by organizing ideas into larger units. For example, in this chapter, dinosaur and other animal footprints will be used to demonstrate reasoning through classification and analogy. Moving from concrete footprints as evidence to abstract analogies, students will be asked to organize observations into patterns, drawing inferences across and between examples.

Understanding is the key to making sense of abstract concepts. Comprehension grows from a combination of definitions, categories, or metaphors. Ideas begin welling up in the mind from contact with evidence within an analytical framework. Footprints will offer creative teachers an opportunity to experiment with "in-the-box," "out-of-the-box," and "off-the-wall" lessons that encourage students to move to higher levels of understanding.

Meaning

Message   Metaphor

FIGURE 7.1

Phase one of learning and teaching, scrutiny, involves finding and sourcing data. Phase two involves categorization and a search for meaning. Classifying data into distinct categories sharpens definitions and stimulates ideas about causes and correlations.

Comparison and contrast between and among examples forms a major component of conceptual and rational development. In this chapter footprints will be used to stimulate thinking about anatomy, evolution, genus, and movement. The footprints send messages that foster classification, a valuable skill for many subjects.

Definitions typically use familiar metaphors and categories to promote further observations that support interpretations of the evidence. Filling in ideas with examples gives depth and meaning that can be applied forever more to new findings. In short, the middle levels of reason.

In-the-Box Lesson

This is a dinosaur footprint petrified into stone over millions of years. The foot probably belonged to an upright two-footed dinosaur that was a predator named Gigandipus. Note that there are three toes and one side or back toe, one clearly showing a toenail. This was a moderately sized animal that could probably move quite quickly. The rest of the body has not been discovered. All we have are these tracks found in a dry riverbed in Utah. The find has been roughly dated to 70 million years ago.

Questions:

1. What kind of footprint is this?
2. Why is it preserved?
3. What type of animal made the footprint?
4. Can you describe the features of the foot?
5. What other animals might make a similar footprint?

Out-of-the-Box Lesson

This footprint was probably made by a dinosaur and is estimated to be about 70 million years old. The footprint, along with many others, was discovered in a dry riverbed in the state of Utah, USA. It has been named Gigandipus and was most likely a predator which moved on two feet. It was probably a moderately sized dinosaur whose footprints were petrified in mud

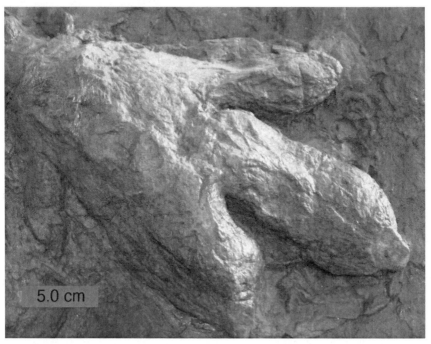

FIGURE 7.2
Gigandipus, a dinosaur footprint in the Lower Jurassic Moenave Formation at the St. George Dinosaur Discovery Site at Johnson Farm, Southwestern Utah. Photograph taken by Mark A. Wilson (Department of Geology, The College of Wooster). Donated to Wikipedia.

over millions of years, leaving us a clear image of the imprint, just like footprints left in cement. Look at the footprint and count the toes. Get a measuring tool to find out how large the foot was and note that the picture provides you with a line of 5cm as a guide to estimating the size. Also note the shape and structure of the foot.

Questions:

1. What kind of footprint is this, and where was it discovered?
2. What is the size and shape of the print?
3. How many toes are shown: three or four?
4. How did the animal walk? Could it run, swim, fly, jump, and so on? How do you know?

5. What were the likely size and habits of this creature? How can you tell?
6. Are there any living animals that would leave the same kind of print if they ran across mud or sand? Why? Are they related to this dinosaur or totally different? How did you decide?

Off-the-Walls Lesson

Look carefully at this footprint set in stone (note a 5 cm measuring bar is provided in the photo). This is a very old footprint dating back 70 million years, and has been named Gigandipus. The print was probably petrified over millions of years and covered with rocks and mud. It was discovered in southwestern Utah in the USA in an area where many fossils have been found. There are many other footprints in the same area, a dry riverbed in an arid region.

Questions:

1. Why would a footprint like this be found in a dry area?
2. How would you describe the print in size and shape?
3. How many toes can you find in the picture and do they all point forward?
4. What kind of animal would leave prints like these?
5. If you drew a body to match the foot, what would the animal look like?
6. How did the animal probably move, on two feet or four? Quickly or slowly? Why do you think so?
7. Are there other animals, past or present, that would leave footprints like these in sand or mud? Why or why not?
8. What can you tell about animal locomotion, size, and habits from footprints?
9. How reliable are your conclusions from just one fossil? What other evidence would you need to feel more certain about your inferences?
10. Would you keep the animal that belongs to this print as a pet? Why or why not?

FORMULATING DEFINITIONS

Observation, taking information in, was the starting point for our discussions of the "engines" for creative teaching and learning. Collecting information/ data followed by a process of defining terms and building categories forms the next phase of creative teaching and learning.

New footprints may be added to the series at each step to generate a more nuanced definition of "feet" and thinking about their function. For example, a teacher may throw in new footprints that are similar or dissimilar to other dinosaurs, birds, or mammals.

Excerpts from Real Classrooms

S1: It looks like a giant chicken or ostrich or something like that. I would never guess it was a dinosaur, never.

S2: I knew it was a dinosaur right away because it is stone, and it has to be very old since it was fossilized a long time ago. Turning into stone takes a long, long time, millions of years.

S1: Now I see it is stone, but what if it were sand, then it could just be a new imprint, couldn't it?

S3: I guessed you were tricking us (to T) so I pulled out a ruler and figured out that the footprint is really very big, bigger than any bird or animal on earth now, I guess.

S4: If you look very closely at the footprint, I think you can see toenails, and a fourth little claw in back just like a bird, or a reptile we studied. But maybe it was a bird. How do we know, as there is no body attached to the footprint, or do we have any total skeletons?

S1: Yes, birdlike, that's it, but not people like, not like a mammal.

T: How can you tell mammals from birds or dinosaurs?

S2: Well, we are mammals but we walk on twos, but have five toes and five fingers, unless something bad has happened to us. My dog has a paw with five fingers but he can't use them the way we do.

T: Thanks for that information.

S2: And my dog can't really pick things up and runs on all fours, but I think the dinosaur we are looking at ran on twos like us, but has three toes and a hook in back like a huge bird, running bird.

S5: Yeah, J., like a ostrich or emu thing from Australia, or weren't there long ago huge birds that ran and couldn't fly? Maybe birds and reptiles are related, and since dinosaurs were reptiles, right, they are related to birds, though we don't have any left.

S1: It would be fun to have some left like in *Jurassic Park*, but scary. Just small ones would be best.

T: Yes, small ones, and we can look them up and check out their footprints on Wikipedia or YouTube if we like when we get our computers going. There are some nice ones on a desert in Arizona I know about, so let's look later, OK?

S6: I'd like to see what the thing looked like, yes I would.

T: Well, we don't really know totally, only from footprints and bones, rocks and stones.

S7: But we can get a better idea, right? Better and fuller, more of a picture. This thing definitely has a bird foot, not a mammal, because of the hook in back and the nasty-looking toenails. The hook was probably to balance in back when it ran or it's left over from holding on to a tree, hey?

T: Those are some useful insights indeed, and maybe we can play with these ideas . . . and ask ourselves why certain families of creatures, species or genus, have three toes and others five: what's the purpose of five or three? If I show you some new footprints can you tell the animals apart, mammals from dinos? Lizards and birds? What do you think?

S3: We have evolved from different beings, different kinds of animals, but I have to think about the reasons for five or three, and as my friend S2 said, we have five like our dogs and cats, but why is a tough question. Why did the dinos have three, and a small one in back? They could run as fast as we can probably, so it's not clear why.

S4: Well I think the dinosaur prints will look a lot like big birds, but not at all like mammals, not like the fox foot you showed us and not like human feet, though ours are kind of strange compared to dogs or foxes. . . .

(Recorded in a seventh-grade science classroom, New Jersey, October 2011.)

Making Tracks: Analyzing Footprints

Compare the photos in figures 7.3 and 7.4 and add them to the boxed lessons. The moa, a very large extinct bird somewhat like an ostrich, has left tracks that could very well be mistaken for a dinosaur's. The *Meles meles* tracks (that's a badger) show differentiation between front and back paws, with five toes all pointed forward. The moa and dinosaur show three toes pointed forward with a spur in back. Why three or five toes? Which creatures

FIGURE 7.3
Moa footprints, from "Footprints of the Moa," by K. Wilson, *Transactions of the Royal Society of New Zealand* (1912), Plate 2, p. 89, http://rsnz.natlib.govt.nz/image/rsnz_45/rsnz_45_00_0229_0000f_ac_01.html.

seem to have a palm? Do they all have a kind of a palm? Do all have toenails? Why or why not?

Do humans have finger- and toenails? Do we really need them? Which of the footprints are we related to and how can you tell? Why do some creatures have similar feet (all four) while others have kinds of hands and feet? Let's talk it over and get our categories clarified and reasons sorted out.

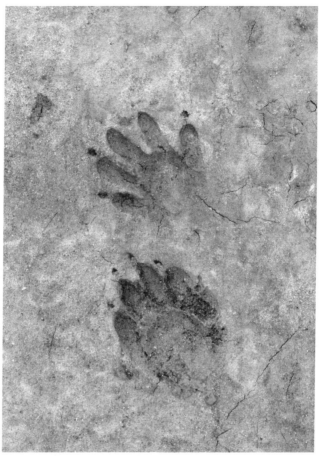

FIGURE 7.4
Badger footprints.

BUILDING CATEGORIES

Building categories and formulating definitions are often overlooked in teaching but are vitally important for basic comprehension. Learners need time to organize data into sets with commonalities and differences, grouping huge quantities of information into easily identifiable categories and patterns. Teachers often treat definitions as though they were "facts," but they actually are concepts. Even a seemingly simple distinction like "city and country" can cause a good deal of confusion, particularly in a nation where suburbs proliferate. Distinguishing among city, suburb, and countryside can raise interesting questions about these three categories and where to draw the lines between them. Simply providing rigid definitions of city, country, and suburb closes off discussion of how human beings in many cultures organize settlements. Where city leaves off and suburbs begin is a subject worthy of investigation in its own right, and may reveal many insights. In addition, definitions can change with the times.

Similarly, if a teacher is still using an older view of the distinction between a virus and a bacterium and not keeping up with new research, students will emerge from school behind the times. Keeping definitions open and renegotiable is a wonderful way of encouraging students to keep their minds open to new data and changing views. Over the course of a semester or year, a creative teacher should frequently revisit definitions to test and retest students' grasp of these ideas.

The process of definition involves creating analogies and building categories by comparing and contrasting. Just as science classifies living things into phyla, families, species, and so on, every learner classifies ideas in every subject. Where definitions have never been examined or revised, students and teachers usually have a very limited grasp and may stumble badly when faced with data that do not fit the definition.

DEVELOPING EXPLANATIONS

The next stage involves building and testing comparisons. Footprints of dinosaurs, for example, may be compared with those of birds and mammals to provoke discussion about similarities and differences. Interpretations begin to be constructed and tested by students. Powerful ideas emerge that can be used to explain and organize the material. Comparisons lead to generalizations about larger and larger quantities of information. Rules, theories, and hypotheses emerge as inquiry proceeds.

To the students these ideas are original in the sense that they've never "discovered" them before. Their own observations, reasoning, and insight led to these theories. Students may never have examined any footprints before, and most certainly not a dinosaur's! Students begin to see that dinosaur feet may leave impressions very similar to those of birds, but not quite like those of mammals. This provokes new inquiries into the evolution of three- or five-toed creatures (humans among them). Questions may be posed about size, shape, function, speed, balance, and adaptation to different environments.

Let's consider another example, this one drawn from history. Students may have a rudimentary knowledge of the American and French Revolutions. Digging deeper into each, learners discover similarities and differences, but can't explain them. They see that the causes and results are quite different. Comparing the two events yields insights into motivations for rebellion, sparking a variety of explanations. Going still higher in the reasoning chain, students may identify general causes of revolutions.

Thus, both the content of study and the reasoning process evolve from close observation with categorization, laying the groundwork for creative leaps of insight.

RECOGNIZING SIMILARITIES AND DIFFERENCES

All of us make analogies. Remember the song from *Sesame Street*? "Which of these things belong together, which of these are really the same?" Herein lies the genesis of simple analogies for the youngest on up to complex comparisons for more mature folks. They come into play in virtually any field and any topic.

Deep within analogies are questions about categories. Scientific theories have been built on categories, ranging from the elements in chemistry to genus and species in biology. Categories are a very important means of organizing, thus providing a sense of order.

For teachers, class and category are necessities in every subject. However, class and category also present problems, especially for the creative teacher. All too often, students are provided with ready-made categories and classifications. In effect, they are asked to accept definitions that were untested by them. Most of these categories were invented to make sense of great swaths of information and build manageable divisions.

But categories overlap in the real world, and it is the intersections that make teaching and learning interesting. A "settled" set of categories that is presented as a list of "true" definitions is by its very nature open to questions. Birds fly, fish swim, and mammals run. What does one do with a bat, a flying fish, or an ostrich? For that matter, what exactly is a dinosaur? The footprints look like a chicken's, perhaps a giant chicken. So were they birds, or lizards? To answer this, teachers need analogies.

DIALOGUES WITH DEFINITIONS: DEVELOPING EXPLANATIONS USING LOGIC AND EVIDENCE

Explanations grow out of a rich mix of data, definitions, and reasoning. Learners begin to deal with the "why," attempting to locate the causes and consequences of phenomena, including human actions. They also begin to understand the origins of and influences on their ideas, why they hold certain loyalties, affections, and biases. Many will realize they've seen *Jurassic Park* too many times!

Where definitions raise questions of meaning, such as the meaning of "war," explanations seek to specify the factors that lead to conflicts. It is relatively easy to define a plant as opposed to an animal, but pinpointing why plants and animals have arisen to fit ecological niches is much more difficult. The value of explanation is in applying data and concepts to determine underlying causes and identify correlations.

Why dinosaur footprints are so similar to those of birds and not so much to those of mammals calls for explanation and may ignite scientific interest as theories are sought to answer the question. Reasons may follow a few forms and patterns, deductive and inductive, correlative and causal, but the goal is always to grasp why things work, why our world behaves in particular ways. With reasons we are able to express and explain the factors that determine an observed outcome.

EXPLANATIONS AS EUREKA!

A "eureka!" is an insight growing out of deep knowledge, comparisons, and meaningful definitions of terms. After studying many geometric shapes, for example, we begin to see patterns and formulas that we didn't understand. The formulae for shapes begin to take on new meaning, leading to generalizations about triangles, squares, circles, and rectangles. We then recombine forms to create, and understand, much more complex polyhedrons and parallelograms and begin to think in three dimensions.

Learned mathematical concepts have enabled insight into the reasons behind formulae and applications. Analysis permits and encourages extensions to new combinations and areas. The process of extending ideas and building on comparisons is the beginning of insight. Theory develops, and inferences grow; all are signs that reasons have been fused into a general concept of a whole class of data. The value of a category—"feet," "revolution," "triangle"—is its

TEXTBOX 7.1

BONUS BOX

Bring standard and large sheets of poster-size paper to class. Ask students to use the small sheets to outline their hands in ink or pencil. Then ask them to take a shoe off and draw their foot. Play show and tell: do hands match feet, or are they different? Why? Do all limbs have five digits, or do any have three? What does this prove? Humans are related more to dinosaurs or to mammals? For extra credit grab a dog or cat (if they sit still that long) and draw their feet, or find a chimpanzee or monkey to cooperate and draw their limbs. Or look online, safer! What will you discover?

FIGURE 7.5
Mystery dinosaur
footprints.

application to examples, new and old. Each new application then provides a test for a concept/definition and alternative explanations.

Eureka happens when learners/teachers grasp a wide array of examples, achieving insights into deeper causes and effects. In many fields, insightful observations, like Darwin's, have changed our understanding of events, but classroom speculations are undervalued. Even if students "discover" an observation that has already been made, they are still using higher-order thinking to arrive at that conclusion.

Students or teachers who experience a eureka have achieved a better level of understanding. This level is often referred to as meta-cognition and is composed of two stages: first, declarative knowing, "knowing that," and second, procedural knowing, "knowing how." The first stage is largely based on evidence and definition; the second stage on theories and methods for obtaining evidence.

Creative learners and teachers begin to know how to know, consciously identifying the skills and procedures of investigation. This is a very high level of understanding, a point where difficult questions are posed about "how anyone knows anything," and "how may truth be determined?"

Thus, at the middle level of thinking creatively, knowledge and method become consciously questioned in the search for better explanations.

REFERENCES

Byrne, R. M. J. 2005. *The Rational Imagination: How People Create Alternatives to Reality.* Cambridge, MA: MIT Press.

Egan, K. 1992. *Imagination in Teaching and Learning.* Chicago: University of Chicago Press.

Frye, N. 1963. *The Educated Imagination.* Toronto: Canadian Broadcasting Corporation.

Norman, R. 2000. *Cultivating Imagination in Adult Education.* Proceedings of the 41st Annual Adult Education Research Conference.

Sutton-Smith, B. 1988. *In Search of the Imagination.* In *Imagination and Education,* edited by K. Egan and D. Nadaner. New York: Teachers' College Press.

Investigations Stimulated

From Puzzlement to Perplexity, Grasping the Mysterious

"The answer is never the answer. What's really interesting is the mystery. If you seek the mystery instead of the answer, you'll always be seeking. I've never seen anybody really find the answer—they think they have, so they stop thinking. But the job is to seek mystery, evoke mystery, plant a garden in which strange plants grow and mysteries bloom. The need for mystery is greater than the need for an answer."

—Ken Kesey, *One Flew Over the Cuckoo's Nest*

"The most beautiful thing we can experience is the mysterious. It is the source of all true art and all science. He to whom this emotion is a stranger, who can no longer pause to wonder and stand rapt in awe, is as good as dead: his eyes are closed.

—Albert Einstein

INTRODUCTION

Creative teachers employ the engine of mystery to present problems as unsolved: perplexing, inconsistent, and confusing.

Cases require a search for clues, a critical eye for anomalies, and a need for testing hypotheses that seek to "solve" problems. Mysteries promote a strong sense of engagement based on curiosity and recognition that something is "amiss" (Larson 2004).

Mysteries typically invite investigation because participants want to fill in the missing pieces (Duckworth 2006). Or they may have the pieces of the puzzle, but these are disorganized and have to be fitted together into a coherent whole. Finally, even if the victory of a complete puzzle is achieved, there may be different theories or hypotheses about causes and effects, competing explanations for the evidence.

Better yet, we may never have it all. Hypotheses may be only partially provable, and unknowns persist until new discoveries are made. Conclusions will remain tentative, in the realm of probabilities. Creative teachers should embrace the tentative and inconclusive because this keeps inquiry going, sustaining intriguing journeys to new discoveries (Bruner 1961).

Unknowns

Puzzles   Hypotheses

FIGURE 8.1

Everyone needs a guide to the perplexed.

Perplexity can be a powerful force in creative teaching. Mastering puzzle design is key to fostering perplexity, as is creating encounters with unknowns and making sense of ambiguity and inconsistency.

To build a sense of perplexity is to arouse student curiosity in its most basic form. Much of the mystery of low pupil interest comes from a lack of the mysterious (Dills 1989). Whatever is to be studied or discussed presents difficulties: unknowns, missing pieces, confusion, and anomalies. While we may, as learners, find mysteries uncomfortable or conflicts upsetting, they arouse our interest. We feel attracted to seeking solutions, fascinated by unsolved problems, gripped by strange anomalies.

Healthy questions arise from perplexity. Challenges develop out of questions that go unanswered.

In the case of mystery, we would very much like to know what's missing, where clues are hidden, and how we work out a solution (if there is one). The process of mystery resembles a good detective story or an archeological dig (Panek 1987). People, artifacts, and stories turn up from many perspectives.

Pieces of the puzzle have to be fitted together to make good deductions. In short, mystery is deeply engaging because we want to know the answers— who, what, where, when, and especially why. Underlying motives and causes are precisely what mystery is about and precisely why it is so interesting.

Mystery as a literary genre is very popular because humans, including the young, enjoy the process of investigation, turning it into a kind of play. Mysteries are like hunts for buried treasure, although the rewards are basically intellectual. We are challenging our minds by evolving and testing new perspectives and new tools of inquiry as we go along.

What *works or fails* excites our imaginations and leads to creative hypothesizing.

PERPLEXITY AND MYSTERY: THE SEARCH FOR CLUES AND CUES

In a mystery strategy, creative teachers have two major choices.

1. They can elect to present problems that are truly mysterious, partially solvable to unsolvable. Such problem mysteries reflect the lack of or confusion inherent in the evidence they rest upon. The material is open to interpretation, even by experts.

2. Teachers can also manufacture mysteries. They accomplish this by reshaping known topics so solutions are hidden or fragmented to create
interesting problems for discussion. The common qualities of the topic are
redesigned for inquiry through the suppression of information.

The first type of "real" mystery is based on real-world evidence and suggests
only tentative solutions. The second type, "manufactured," is based on a
creative teacher's redesign of evidence for pedagogical purposes (Gerwin and
Zevin 2010).

Creating a sense of mystery is key to the whole investigation. This means,
in effect, that teachers must make students feel like detectives searching for
missing evidence, taking part in an elaborate puzzle, creating potential answers or solutions. Quick solutions don't help at all.

Any lesson, any subject, that can be presented as straightforward information can also be presented as mysterious, as perplexing. A mystery permits
both teacher and student to participate in a Sherlock Holmes style of inquiry
in the hope that all of the clues will add up to an "aha!" moment of discovery.
In real life, mysteries are often quite messy, with lots of variables, competing
explanations, and incomplete data files.

As creative teachers, it is the messy versions we want to replicate in our
classrooms. Digging up a mess in an archeology site calls for close scrutiny
of the discoveries. Theories are born, and die, as more evidence is uncovered.
But students may need warm-ups in the form of easier, minor or medium
mysteries before reaching the big time.

A messy mystery is preferred for several reasons: first, it mimics reality.
Second, it teaches patience and observation skills. And third, messy problems
provide students with the opportunity to reinforce their research skills. Observations, hypotheses, and reasoning lead to debating solutions. The process
motivates student investigations.

Seated firmly on a living room couch watching a mystery with friends or
family is fun as you watch and guess who did it. But having someone come
in and "solve" it for you in a few minutes is really aggravating. Problem
solved equals enjoyment killed, and skills untested, especially when promoting learning skills.

That's why Sherlock Holmes, Hercule Poirot, and Miss Marple all generally wait until well toward the end of the show to explain the whodunit
(Murch 1975).

Like these detectives, teachers employing a mystery engine, whether reality-based or invented, have to make sure it lasts awhile! If the mystery is too easy, the solution will occur shortly. The lesson won't be sustained. As a rule in psychology, the more certain and easier a problem is to solve, the less interesting it is likely to be for students (Furth and Wachs 1974). Conversely, uncertain and intriguing problems inspire more inquisitiveness, up to a point!

For students unused to problem-finding and problem-solving, too many unknowns, too much controversy, and too much ambiguity may frustrate them (Alfieri et al. 2011). Their progress will be inhibited. Therefore, for many students, problems must be introduced gradually, with limited clues, limited data, and a small range of conclusions.

As the audience becomes more adept and self-assured as higher-order thinkers, the range and depth of evidence, of perplexity, may be increased. With practice, audiences will become far better observers and clue collectors, generating solutions from evidence (Adelson 2004).

As a fine mystery draws us in, so may a creative teacher draw us out of being "boxed in."

MISSING PIECES AND MISMATCHED PARTS

One technique for stimulating perplexity is to offer evidence that is incomplete. In a well-designed mystery, data is missing, damaged, misleading, or confusing. For example, when archeologists uncover a new find—a tomb several thousand years old—they may discover artifacts whose function is unclear.

After searching for other clues using carbon dating, writing or symbols, related objects, placement, and numbers, scientists work out an educated guess that best fits the facts. They might be right or wrong about their hypotheses, but they at least make a convincing case.

Archeologists may also find a complete tomb, but with everything fallen in, disturbed by an earthquake, or ransacked by grave robbers. Pieces that were once together have come apart and, much like a puzzle, have to be reassembled. There are mismatches to play with and rearrange. Evidence must be formed into a coherent whole based on hypotheses.

Sometimes mistakes can be made, particularly when parts are unusual or unfamiliar. Alternative hypotheses develop to explain the finds, lending an air of controversy to discoveries. Researchers disagree about the clues, and the conclusions, providing ideas and interpretations to think over.

No one really knows which hypothesis is best, but as more finds are discovered and analyzed, scientists build a series of inferences. Eventually they can "explain" the function of the artifact, but truthfully, its function is never really known with total surety. Unfortunately, hypotheses that are partially proven are presented in many textbooks as "true," or accepted, siphoning off any sense of mystery for audiences.

A second technique is to redesign, actually deconstruct or reconstruct, a standard lesson so it draws students into a problem. In this situation, teachers already know the evidence, and the solution, but are trying to find ways to make the topic more engaging.

For example, a science teacher might like to have students think about the topic of phototropism, how plants seek light to grow. An experiment can be created allowing plants to "move" in the direction of greater light sources. Even better if this experiment can be presented dramatically using plant covers with light holes. Students must predict the direction and intensity of growth without seeing the plants. Later, they check hypotheses by removing the covers.

The teacher can simply tell students about this phenomenon or use a text. But it might be a lot more fun to perplex students by hands-on demonstrations using their own plants. As an added mystery, leave one plant under cover totally, and another with a single opening in the pot, keeping both watered. Ask students to predict outcomes.

Creative teachers hope for bold and imaginative detectives who make predictions.

Thus mystery can grow out of actual unknowns, lost pieces of the puzzle, or from creative "constructions" redesigned for multiple interpretations (Zevin and Gerwin 2010). Creative teachers need only exploit the characteristics of the evidence to build a sense of perplexity. They can sustain the lesson with clues and cues from the data, and by adding expert theories for study. Audience findings can be compared and contrasted with those of the expert detectives.

Confirmation reassures audiences; contradictions upset them. But either way, mystery goes a long way toward promoting active involvement with evidence. Teachers create perplexity where it did not exist before by omitting or rearranging information. The overlooked and familiar suddenly seems fascinating. Introducing a mystery object provokes new interest and new meanings develop.

Everyone likes playing detective, especially as hypotheses develop and tentative solutions evolve!

CONTRADICTIONS, INCONSISTENCIES, AND AMBIGUITIES

Perplexity and a sense of mystery may also arise from contradictions, inconsistencies, and ambiguities within or between data.

Across every subject and discipline, there are examples of data, evidence, and textbook materials that, upon close analysis, raise questions about meaning and message. Just as portions may seem missing or illogically arranged, there are even more complicated problems possible (Raths et al. 1967).

These problems comprise three main areas: first, there are contradictions perceived. Authors seem to contradict their own statements, or the work of others. To continue with our archeology metaphor, scientists may not agree on the meaning of the findings; some may give greater importance to some parts than to others. Some may contradict themselves by changing tone or conclusions. The experts may also argue with each other's interpretations of the evidence, leading to a full-scale debate.

That is great for creative classrooms!

Second, a text, argument, or hypothesis may reveal inconsistencies, bits and pieces of facts don't match, or chains of reasoning go in different directions. Evidence may go against the main points. Learners and teachers need to check for inconsistencies and render a judgment about the validity and reliability of evidence. If there are too many inconsistencies perhaps certain data should be downgraded in value, and other more consistent reports upgraded.

Third, there are problems of interpretation due to ambiguities. Readers, observers, and participants are not quite sure what the main points are or how authors came to conclusions. Purposes seem vague or confusing. Some reasoning seems to be left out, terms are not clearly defined, conclusions are unsupported, and so on.

So far, contradictions, inconsistencies, and ambiguities sound like material you would want to avoid in your classroom. But variations are powerful forces working to build perplexity. Each presents problems to students who must hone their skills of reading, observing, and listening in order to develop their own ideas.

By adding to a sense of perplexity, ambiguities and inconsistencies push the learner to expend much more energy thinking up a solution. Higher-order thinking would be far less probable in a linear lesson that lays out all the steps and makes sure of a "correct" conclusion. Practice drawing and defending inferences, and critically analyzing data, leads to more attentive listening and reading across all subjects and sources.

In effect, we are teaching students to approach what they are learning with powerful skills of analysis and synthesis. Deep observation is enhanced by mystery tools of investigation, tools that probe material with greater scrutiny and a heightened sense of potential imperfection.

Through perplexity, students become critical consumers of information rather than simply collectors.

THE MAGIC OF MYSTERY: PERPLEXITY AND PROBLEM-FINDING/SOLVING

In Mesopotamia gods were thought to be physically present in the materials and experiences of daily life. Enlil, considered the most powerful Mesopotamian god during most of the third millennium B.C., was a "raging storm" or "wild bull," while the goddess Inanna reappeared in different guises as the morning and evening star. Deities literally inhabited their cult statues after they had been animated by the proper rituals, and fragments of worn statues were preserved within the walls of the temple.

This standing figure, with clasped hands and a wide-eyed gaze, is a worshiper. It was placed in the "Square Temple" at Tell Asmar, perhaps dedicated to the god Abu, in order to pray perpetually on behalf of the person it represented. For humans equally were considered to be physically present in their statues. Similar statues were sometimes inscribed with the names of rulers and their families.

A "Real" Mystery Lesson in Three Versions

Studying ancient history or art history allows us to look at many strange and curious paintings, sculptures, friezes, and buildings. Rather than simply telling what we know about a mystery object, why not present it for speculation concerning its origins, time period, function, style, materials, and placement?

The statue presented above is a fairly typical statue from ancient Sumer, one of the first "civilized" areas that gave rise to some of the earliest known statuary, agriculture, cities, states, and writing. Archeologists and historians

FIGURE 8.2
Babylonian votive figure of god, standing male worshiper,
2750–2600 B.C. Mesopotamia, Eshnunna (modern Tell Asmar).
Alabaster (gypsum), shell, black limestone, bitumen; H 29.5 cm.
Fletcher Fund, 1940 (40.156).

know a great deal about Sumer because we have learned how to read their
cuneiform writing. Many objects have been uncovered and cities discovered.

But many of the objects found do not always have a clear interpretation.
For example, our friend here has been described by two captions, "a votive
figure" and then as a "standing male worshiper." The first description is

rather vague and most students will have to run to look up "votive," while the second is perhaps too precise, focusing on three details without understanding the whole.

A major issue is that the photographer and archeologist are solving the mystery for you by drawing inferences and labeling an object for you. They have already decided what it is all about, without giving the observer/learner a chance for close scrutiny. Since we already have two captions, we can have many more, and truthfully, much is *not* known.

For example, the style is not discussed, nor the rather elaborate beard. The pose is discussed but not the overall effect, nor where the figure is looking. The point is that a mystery gives students the chance for their own interpretation before the experts rush in to explain. We need some challenging questions to get a discussion started, particularly questions that draw parallels between our own lives and the past.

If an object is totally foreign, how can we understand it at all? So this makes a partially constructed and partially real mystery. Perhaps not so difficult as a "new" find that the experts argue over (though that would be healthy for students who seek more of a challenge).

In the Box: Mystery Questions
1. What features of the statue do you find most striking? Do any features impress you as mysterious? Why?
2. Why does the figure keep his hands together in the manner shown? Can you imitate that pose? Do the pose and the hands remind of you anything you do? How big is 29.5 centimeters?
3. Why is he wearing a gown? Is there a shirt? Why are the eyes so wide open? Is this person like us or not like us? If we dressed him in a suit could we tell where or when he was from?
4. Where and when do you think this figure was sculpted? What was its purpose? Do you think he was a real person or a symbol?
5. Do you think the figure was worshiping or was worshiped? How can you decide?

Out of the Box: Mystery Questions
1. Are there any present-day analogs to this statue? Do people still make statues? Why? What purpose do statues serve?

2. What might an archeologist or scientist ask about the statue that we might not think of to help them understand it? What additional information would we most like to have about the statue and the people who made it?
3. Can anyone make a statue "out of their time" or do all statues and art represent their times and places?
4. Do behaviors and poses last through the ages and mean the same thing, like prayer?
5. As we go back in time and across lands, would objects we find be more or less difficult to interpret? Why? Are there still mysteries?

Off the Walls: Mystery Questions
1. Does art follow prayer? Does prayer follow art?
2. Why do people use their hands and faces to express belief?
3. How can you decide meaning and message from the distant past, from a culture no longer with us?
4. Do analogies work? Can you interpret the past from the present or the present from the past? Why or why not?
5. Is the picture below a match or analog to the ancient statue? Why or why not? What is the man sitting in front of? Why?
6. Can you find pictures of your own that show people using their hands and bodies to do work and express feelings?

FIGURE 8.3

What makes mystery (as long as teacher doesn't run in and conveniently solve a problem) so powerful is its association with search and find behavior. But teachers must make and treat a mystery with respect for the investigation and the outcomes. It is students, learners, viewers who need the experience of searching for clues, putting these together, and drawing conclusions. It is the teacher who acts as a facilitator for investigation and an arranger or designer or chooser of the curriculum material being studied.

A sense of perplexity can be frustrating, but also exciting. There is a tension between both psychological states that drives inquiry. Human beings really enjoy exploration and discovery. We are willing to be fed information and led to conclusions, but this does not have the inherent excitement of boating in what is for us uncharted waters.

Mystery/perplexity is a label provided for creative teaching strategies that promote thinking outside the box and off the walls.

We may complain about problems but also enjoy solving them. In formal classrooms, problems are usually academic, repetitive, and predetermined by local, state, or national curriculum requirements. Students are a passive audience on the whole from childhood through adulthood, receiving rather than producing knowledge and insights.

In a mystery setting, students become active participants in the process of collecting and making sense of data. Up to a point, they are the ones seeking clues, comparing sources, and creating hypotheses to explain and understand the content. And, if we encourage them, they are the ones to draw the final conclusions from the information. To do a thoughtful and careful job on any set of data, they must be aware of what is missing, inaccurate, and inconsistent as well as what is proposed, claimed, and asserted.

Excerpts from Real Classrooms

(Group representatives report their findings about the Sumerian statuette)

T: Well, you've all had a few minutes to look at the statue and analyze its features, so are we ready for reports of hypotheses? Remember, hypotheses are open to argument, these are your interpretations of the statue, not necessarily true? So go for it . . .

G1: My group did not agree totally, but most of us thought that it was definitely a man, and he was praying, not exactly like we do, but prayerful. Hands clasped. Long beard, gown, bug-eyed, trance, maybe.

G2: My group also did not agree but think he is praying, but we had an argument over who or what he was, priest, king, leader, just a person, etc. It is hard to tell because he is dressed simply except for that long beard, and has no crown or other items you might think are royal or noble. We all definitely saw this as religious, but not sure who or what he was praying to.

G3: People look relaxed and "out of it" when they are praying because they are trying to go beyond the real world to communicate with gods or god or something. He seems to be like that because of those bug eyes, and dizzy look, and the long gown, it's a dress!

G4: We really felt we cannot be sure, after all, the thing is thousands of years old and how are we supposed to know what they thought? Maybe we are reading into this statue our own values and feelings? Maybe he is on drugs? Maybe he is a god himself and others are worshiping him? Maybe, a lot of maybes. This is not an easy assignment.

S1 (breaks in): Yes we don't know enough . . . there are too many unknowns.

T: Well, give it a chance, and let's hear from other groups first, OK?

G5: We saw this statue as put in a church, like an offering to the saints. People might have had these made to bring to church for a service or maybe the statues represent passed away family members or the churchgoer who leaves himself standing there asking for blessings. It was religious, we all felt, but from long ago. You gave us that Hindu man praying and that was not exactly like the statue but it is now and not so different, so we all felt that this has great religious meaning even if we can't understand it completely.

S1/G5 (breaks in): You know, in digging up the past you can't always be sure of how to make sense of what you find; that's why it's a mystery. But here we need more to go on, like books, other finds in the area, pictures of other statues, men, women, children, etc., before we can make really great conclusions about—

T: You are out of turn, but those are excellent insights and maybe you would like to take the lead in looking for more evidence, OK? . . .

(Ninth grade, NYC, April 2010, Global History 1)

Dealing with Perplexity

Perplexity eventually yields understanding, but not always. In some cases we are still perplexed, or perhaps partially so. Yet real life is not always clear-cut, and we need skills of interpretation and comprehension to pull us through difficult problems and issues. A creative teacher can provide these skills through mystery and related strategies that help learners practice synthesizing evidence and evaluating hypotheses.

It is the creative teacher's role to break down and build up the many complex steps in mystery. A teacher must know her audience and tailor the mystery activities to just a bit beyond their current levels of knowledge and skills. That is, the mystery must challenge but not deeply frustrate.

The mystery should admit of several solutions, paced to reinforce and reward participants along the way with insights and understandings. All conclusions should not be left to the very end, but there should be many clues to pick up along the way. Contradictions and inconsistencies need identification, but if the material is too dense, difficult, and ambiguous, this may inhibit the overall effect rather than enhance the mystery.

A REAL MYSTERY

Olmec culture was unknown to historians until the mid-19th century. In 1869 the Mexican antiquarian traveller José Melgar y Serrano published a description of the first Olmec monument to have been found in situ. This monument—the colossal head now labeled Tres Zapotes Monument A—had been discovered in the late 1850s by a farm worker clearing forested land on a hacienda in Veracruz. Hearing about the curious find while travelling through the region, Melgar y Serrano first visited the site in 1862 to see for himself and complete the partially exposed sculpture's excavation. His description of the object, published several years later after further visits to the site, represents the earliest documented report of an artifact of what is now known as the Olmec culture.

In the latter half of the 19th century, Olmec artifacts such as the Kunz Axe came to light and were subsequently recognized as belonging to a unique artistic tradition.

If you read this text from Wikipedia or from any study of the Olmec, you will probably come away quite dissatisfied. The Olmec, you will find out, were the first known Mesoamerican civilization with towns, a distinct artistic tradition, agriculture, and a settled lifestyle that included a ball game something like basketball they bequeathed to all subsequent Mesoamerican peoples. As far as we can tell, they began forming settlements as early as 2500 B.C. but emerged as a powerful culture after about 1500 B.C. and lasted until about 400 B.C. That's a

FIGURE 8.4
Ancient Olmec jade: Oaxaca, Mexico. The famous Kunz Axe, reportedly found in the hills of Oaxaca in 1890. Named after George Kunz, this votive axe was one of the first artifacts to be identified with the Olmec civilization. The end comes to an edge, although it is very doubtful that the axe ever served more than a ritual function. Photo by Madman/Free licensing from Wikipedia.

long time, but the interesting part of this mystery is they were really discovered only in the nineteenth century and had no writing system we know of, but left a good deal of rather strange objects, sculptures, and art.

So if you want to try out a series of real archeological mysteries, use Olmec objects for class discussion in ancient history, art, or perhaps science. These items will give everyone a run for their money in trying to interpret meaning, message, and function. For example, turn to the "axe," if that is what it was, and try to figure out its message.

Like the Sumerian statue we see again the word "votive," a favorite of archeological authors, apparently, meaning that something is perhaps religious in purpose. This is fine, but fails to tell us why the "axe" is made of a precious stone, jade, or why the being on it seems partly animal and partly human. Maybe it is a child, maybe not? Maybe it was presented as art or as religion? Maybe it was private or maybe it was public? Maybe we don't know. So try this out with a group of creative inquirers and see what they infer. Ask them to write stories about the object and share these with each other.

Direct them to do some research on the Olmec, look at other objects, and read a few easier-to-acquire archeological views. By the end, everyone, if they're honest, might see the Olmec and this jade "axe" as quite a mystery, learning that it is not easy to solve. Particularly where written language is absent, the mystery is more difficult. Then take a look at secondary sources and enjoy the many, sometimes fanciful, interpretations of the experts.

Mystery Questions
1. Why does it have the shape of a dagger or hatchet? What is in the mouth? Teeth, tongue, something else entirely?
2. Was this piece the work of a skillful and accomplished artist, who used the stone to make it beautiful? How can you decide?
3. What does the figure mean? How was it used? Where was it placed? Is this something ordinary or extraordinary, then or now? How can you tell?
4. Why are prehistoric or ancient or sometimes even modern artifacts difficult to interpret? What would we like to know that might help us figure out the mystery?
5. If you met the people who created and used the "axe" what might they believe or think about their world? Can you make any safe or even risky predictions about their beliefs and behaviors?

6. Are people still making things like this? Are we still concerned with religion? Do you think this represents a belief in the supernatural? Why or why not?

SUMMARY AND CONCLUSIONS

Thus, a mystery lesson should provide sufficient data and clues to promote inquiry, but not so much that the audience will easily achieve a solution. There must be a balance between the information provided and the potential for solution.

If the mystery is "manufactured" for classroom inquiry, clues should be selected to stimulate multiple explanations and insights, although students may eventually converge on a "most acceptable" conclusion. In the case of a real mystery, where origins, causes, and inferences are subject to contested interpretations, the creative teacher needs to select enough examples, and background expertise, to promote sound interpretations. Later, a range of secondary expertise, such as scholars, textbooks, and scientists, should be offered to help learners confirm, deny, or enrich their hypotheses.

Designing mystery lessons requires experimentation and practice. Over time comfort with provocative or unusual questions, detective work, will grow as audiences learn how to approach mysteries. Actresses/actors and audience will come together in enjoyment and intellectual stimulation that perhaps might equal experiencing a good mystery novel or film. In effect, mystery will help shift the epistemology of learning from collecting facts to practicing skills of inquiry.

For example, when the question of global warming comes up, there are assertions and denials about its validity that need careful checking. Global warming is a "mystery" that needs investigation, and raises many questions across a wide path of disciplines. The viewpoints surrounding global climate change are quite perplexing in range and intensity, presenting a second mystery of clashing interpretations and values. It takes a creative teacher to prepare people to deal with a serious investigation of global warming and related issues.

Thus, mystery strategies help learners become familiar with perplexity, and how to deal with it. Comfort with perplexity, perhaps even enthusiasm for it, bolsters students as they work through problems all across the school curriculum and throughout life.

BONUS BOX: A "CONSTRUCTED" MYSTERY LESSON ON GEOGRAPHY

To illustrate the principles in this chapter, let's provide students with a mystery map drawn to their specifications. Instead of complex modern maps with too many variables, let's provide a nice group of upper elementary or middle school youngsters a hand-drawn map of a "mystery" area. Let's delete all identifying

FIGURE 8.5

names, places, and human-made work. Show the place just as it was when it was created, giving landforms, climate, vegetation, and waterways. That's probably enough for young learners.

Next, let's pose a fairly difficult question: if you were exploring this property, and had no former claims on it (though there were a variety of folks living there), where would you decide to build three or four key cities? What factors would be important? What factors are important for any city, especially medium-sized to big ones? Form groups and have the class decide on their locations, share answers, and discuss which most likely had the best choices defended by the best reasons.

Next, the lesson can be extended into a mystery unit about plant growth.

Groups can be given plants to care for and grow in black boxes, some with tiny windows, others with large windows, cut open in different directions. They may be asked to keep a log of plant development, noting direction, foliage growth, health, and size. Some plants can be kept far from light sources, others near. Rather than give conclusions about phototropism, the creative teacher engages students by perplexing and challenging them with hands-on investigations.

REFERENCES

Adelson, R. 2004. "Instruction vs. Exploration in Science Learning." APA Online, *Monitor on Psychology*, 35:6.

Alfieri, L., P. J. Brooks, N. J. Aldrich, and H. R. Tenenbaum. 2011. "Does Discovery-based Instruction Enhance Learning?" *Journal of Educational Psychology* 103 (1): 1–18.

Bruner, J. S. 1961. "The Act of Discovery." *Harvard Educational Review* 31 (1): 21–32.

Dills, L. 1989. *The Mystery of the Passive Students*, vol. 4. New Haven, CT: Yale-New Haven Teachers Institute and Yale University Press.

Duckworth, E. 2006. *The Having of Wonderful Ideas and Other Essays on Teaching and Learning*. New York: Teachers College Press.

Furth, H. G., and H. Wachs. 1974. *Thinking Goes to School: Piaget's Theory in Practice*. New York: Oxford University Press.

Gerwin, D., and J. Zevin. 2010. *Teaching US History as Mystery*. New York: Routledge.

Larson, J. 2004. *Bringing Mysteries Alive for Children and Young Adults*. Santa Barbara, CA: ABC-CLIO and Linworth Publishing.

Murch, A. E. 1975. *The Development of the Detective Novel*. London: Peter Owen Limited.

Panek, L. L. 1987. *An Introduction to the Detective Story*. Bowling Green, OH: Bowling Green State University Popular Press.

Raths, L. E., et al. 1967. *Teaching for Thinking, Theory and Application*. Columbus, OH: Charles E. Merrill.

Zevin, J., and D. Gerwin. 2010. *Teaching World History as Mystery*. New York: Routledge.

Viewpoints Explored

Different Perspectives and Conflicting Interpretations

"Two monks were watching a flag flapping in the wind. One said to the other, 'The flag is moving.' The other replied, 'The wind is moving.' [The Master] Huineng overheard this. He said, 'Not the flag, not the wind, the mind is moving.'"

—Mumon, *The Gateless Gate*

INTRODUCTION

Creative teachers use viewpoints to explore different perspectives and conflicting interpretations. Viewpoints may reflect converging, contradictory, and conflicting frames of reference. They encourage learners to examine questions from different vantage points and check the trustworthiness of eyewitnesses and data sources.

The "engine" of perspective leads to questions about how and why differing viewpoints develop. In a way, perspective is a higher-order version of comparison and contrast. Let's explore perspective by encouraging students to understand different viewpoints and take on the roles of others.

Why is it that people, even in the same circumstances, have such different and varied perceptions of events? How do these views develop? And why

FIGURE 9.1
Satire on False Perspective by William Hogarth (1754), reprinted by William Heath, London (1822).

Converging views

Contradictory views   Conflicting views

FIGURE 9.2

do they differ across a spectrum from a modest little auto accident to deep philosophical disagreement?

Human beings have probably always had their own perspectives based on culture, experience, and personality (Gallagher and Zahavi 2007). But these differ from person to person and profoundly influence how subjects are conceptualized, even what is noticed or overlooked. Differing views define how the world is understood and described, yielding accounts that may be confusing and not fully trustworthy. In something as supposedly straightforward as a news story, the language, details, and overall tone are shaped by the author's personality and ideology, consciously and subconsciously (Doyle 2001). Even relatively "objective" subjects such as math and science offer a range of views, methods, and solutions.

Perspectives reflect different categories: "insiders" vs. "outsiders," "proponents" vs. "opponents." Location, stance, and belonging may make a great deal of difference in interpreting events.

Insider views emanate from a sense of belonging to a special group. These insiders may be privy to information, feelings, skills, and attitudes that outsiders may find difficult to understand. Belonging to a group shapes views of particular events and the world in general. For example, patriotism may blind citizens to information that is clear to others.

Outsiders, by contrast, may have more objective views of events, but lack or fail to appreciate the perspectives of the insiders. For instance, religious beliefs frequently evoke sharply different interpretations and viewpoints. Despite the fact that the three major religions share much in common, their differences produce high levels of misperception and opposition among both insiders and outsiders.

Outsiders may also be overwhelmed by the variety of viewpoints available. Without that insider knowledge, how can they begin to understand a world of multiple, often competing explanations and theories? Particularly when explanations or theories clash and challenge each other's validity.

A STORY ABOUT PERSPECTIVE

Stories are excellent venues for considering viewpoints because every story represents an author's agenda expressed as narrative. Stories are often figurative rather than literal, allegories that demand interpretation. They are an art form, using language in playful, interesting ways to get a point across. The agenda of a story may be unclear or confusing, and this is wonderful for creative teachers who hope to use stories to promote higher-order thinking.

Read the story that follows. Whose viewpoint does it represent? Why do the characters each seem to tell a different tale? Why do the facts of the story seem to vary by character? What about the newspaper account at the end? What really happened? Is one of the characters more reliable than the others? Is the story meant to be funny or serious, and just how do you decide? Does the style of writing give you any clues?

What would you say is the tale's agenda, if any?

What is Averchenko, the author, saying about perspective?

"Point of View" by A. Averchenko

"Men are comic," she said, smiling dreamily. Not knowing whether this indicated praise or blame, I answered noncommittally: "Quite true." "Really, my husband's a regular Othello. Sometimes I am sorry I married him." I looked helplessly at her. "Until you explain—" I began.

"Oh, I forgot that you haven't heard. About three weeks ago, I was walking home with my husband through the square. I had a large black hat on, which suits me awfully well, and my cheeks were quite pink from walking. As we passed under a street light, a pale, dark-haired fellow standing nearby glanced at me and suddenly took my husband by the sleeve."

"Would you oblige me with a light," he says. Alexander pulled his arm away, stooped down, and quicker than lightning, banged him on the head with a brick. He fell like a log. Awful!"

"Why, what on earth made your husband get jealous all of a sudden?"

She shrugged her shoulders. "I told you men are very comic."

Bidding her farewell, I went out, and at the corner came across her husband. "Hello, old chap," I said. "They tell me you've been breaking people's heads." He burst out laughing. "So, you've been talking to my wife. It was jolly lucky that brick came so pat into my hand. Otherwise, just think: I had about fifteen hundred rubles in my pocket, and my wife was wearing her diamond earrings."

"Do you think he wanted to rob you?"

"A man accosts you in a deserted spot, asks for a light and gets hold of your arm. What more do you want?"

Perplexed, I left him and walked on.

"There's no catching you today," I heard a voice say from behind.

I looked around and saw a friend I hadn't set eyes upon for three weeks.

"Lord, I exclaimed. "What on earth has happened to you?"

He smiled faintly and asked in turn: "Do you know whether any lunatics have been at large lately? I was attacked by one three weeks ago. I left the hospital only today."

With sudden interest, I asked: "Three weeks ago? Were you sitting in the square?"

"Yes, I was. The most absurd thing. I was sitting in the square, dying for a smoke. NO matches! After ten minutes or so, a gentleman passed with some old hag. He was smoking. I go up to him, touch him on the sleeve and ask in my most polite manner: 'Can you oblige me with a light?' And what do you think? The madman stoops down, picks up something, and the next moment I am lying on the ground with a broken head, unconscious. You probably read about it in the newspapers."

I look up and asked earnestly: "Do you really believe you met up with a lunatic?"

"I am sure of it."

Anyhow, afterwards I was eagerly digging in old back numbers of the local paper. At last I found what I was looking for: A short note in the accident column.

UNDER THE INFLUENCE OF DRINK

"YESTERDAY MORNING, THE KEEPERS OF THE SQUARE FOUND ON A BENCH A YOUNG MAN WHOSE PAPERS SHOW HIM TO BE OF GOOD FAMILY. HE HAD EVIDENTLY FALLEN TO THE GROUND WHILE IN A STATE OF EXTREME INTOXICATION, AND BROKEN HIS HEAD ON A NEARBY BRICK. THE DISTRESS OF THE PRODIGAL'S PARENTS IS INDESCRIBABLE."

This story demands close reading as an exercise in figuring out point of view. It is both intriguing and amusing. Tales can be used in many contexts to stimulate imagination in and out of the box, see below.

THREE LESSONS USING AVERCHENKO'S STORY

In the Box
1. Why does the author say, "All men are comic?"
2. Does he mean only men, or women too?
3. What is the story about? What is the man's story, the wife's story, the newspaper story?
4. Do all stories match or is each view different?
5. Why are there such different versions of this little incident?
6. Is the author making fun of people or newspapers?
7. What is the author's viewpoint?

Out-of-the-Box Lesson
1. Do you personally think "all men are comic?"
2. If you had to write your own newspaper report using all the versions in this story, how would you present the truth?

3. When people witness an event, are their reports reliable? What kinds of events make people more or less reliable?
4. Is there anyone in this story whose account you would especially trust? Why?
5. Does the author make fun of people or newspapers or all of us?
6. Do you think this story is funny or serious? How can you tell?

Off-the-Walls Lesson
1. What is a "point of view?"
2. Do you have a point of view? Does everyone have a point of view or are some people pointless?
3. How does a point of view work for you? Does it help you to see things as they are or as you would like them to be, or something else entirely?
4. How do you explain the characters' accounts: man, woman, husband, and newspaper? Do they match each other? Why or why not?
5. Would you trust your own description of an auto accident? A disagreement about money? A social issue of great importance?
6. Do you think people can trust each other's point of view? If not, how can we tell truth from fiction? If yes, why?
7. Does viewpoint always add up to humor or can it lead to tragedy as well?
8. Could you rewrite the story as a tragedy?
9. If you could ask the author one big question, what would you pose?

Clearly, the idea of perspective has inherently challenging qualities.

Examining differences and similarities allows students to identify varied views and gain insights into the reasons these views developed. Perceptions are based on experience, ideology, and history. In a classroom, analyzing perspectives will provoke a large number of questions and fruitful discussion and build a floor for creative insights (Perkins 2000).

EXCERPTS FROM REAL CLASSROOMS

Teacher: What do you think this story means?

S1: It's all about how newspapers screw up news, I think.

S2: Yes, but it's really about how people screw up what they say to each other.

S3: Stories don't match.

S4: Well, I think it's really a joke, making fun of everyone, like a game. Can anyone tell the truth?

T: Is it about truth or point of view?

S5: Well both, can't it be both? Everyone has their view, but we don't always communicate so well with each other.

S3: Yeah, we don't so much lie as just only know our own story of events.

T: But isn't that a big problem? If everyone tells their own story, and they don't match, then what?

S1: Then we have to play mix and match to find out who's closest to being right. Like in the story the newspaper was the most wrong, people were better.

S6: Some news is awful, like *The Post*, you can't tell if they're lying to you.

S4: Yeah, but some people are awful too, like "she" in the story. Whoever she was makes up details to suit herself.

S7: Now I am getting upset! I want the answers to this story: there's got to be a truth, a right interpretation, got to . . .

T: Why?

S7: Well there are facts: like that man who just wanted a light for his cigarette in the story, he sounded truthful.

S2: How do you know? The others thought he was going to rob them.

S7: Well, I don't think so. They all sound crazy now. Someone's wrong.

S1: Come on now, it's a story, just a story, but it does sound real.

T: Well do you think all the news is factual or fictional, and is fiction really all just made up?

S4: You are just trying to upset us, and that is "comic" because we really want answers . . .

T: But can we really find answers and does it matter that the story was "made up?" What if it was in a newspaper? You'd all think it was honest truth, right?

S7: Maybe.

S2: Not at all. . . .

(Eleventh grade, language arts classroom, NYC, November 2011)

This strategy also raises the issue of corroboration, the reliability and validity of the evidence. We must decide which, if any, of the viewpoints is most trustworthy. We begin, perhaps, to understand how each is motivated by self-interest, bias, politics, and personal experience. We may be frightened by the possibility that there is no truth.

The study of perspective/points of view is a complex and challenging engine to excite student interest. The process of corroboration is stimulating and rewarding because it is more complex and demanding than more straightforward observation and explanation.

Students must identify and classify views: are the perspectives converging, overlapping, differing distinctly, or conflicting? Does each account have a clear agenda or ideology, or are values ambiguous or hidden?

When using this strategy, considerable attention must be paid to interpretation. It helps if students have partners with whom to share ideas or, better yet, they can work in groups and debate conclusions. How do we meld views together into a coherent whole? What if each view disagrees with the rest: a sort of "Rashomon" effect where every eyewitness has a different story? Can the many viewpoints be fused into a coherent whole?

The complexities and difficulties perspective evokes reinforce interest and stimulate attention. Clashes and arguments generate emotion and bring ideas to light. Horizons are broadened and deepened. Perspective offers huge opportunities for teachers brave enough to help students explore alternatives and step into new frames of reference.

Perspective promotes higher-order thinking across affective, cognitive, and psychomotor dimensions.

POINT OF VIEW: THE MYSTERY OF MANY PERSPECTIVES

As perspectives become more complex, the level of thinking required rises.

Contested or overlapping perspectives in particular offer the challenge of developing criteria to test for "truth." An event as common as an automobile accident can generate many views that agree, disagree, or partially agree. In an accident there are almost always different, though not usually opposite, versions of what happened.

There are, of course, the two drivers and their passengers, if any, as well as bystanders, and police if they were around. Bystanders' views and drivers' views almost always disagree, maybe on minor details, maybe on big conclusions. Who was at fault and what actually happened need to be hammered out.

Accident reports can be fascinating because they almost always demonstrate that perceptions are shaped by standpoints, personal experiences, and ideas of right and wrong, as well as self-protection. Motivations may vary, but usually each driver and bystander shapes a story that serves his or her own best interests and sense of morality.

Often, moral judgments play a big role in how a tale is recounted and what conclusions are drawn. Even the police, who are trained to be objective, may provide descriptions that are contrary to those of drivers and other eyewitnesses. An "ordinary" auto accident may engender quite an array of viewpoints and interpretations that do not fully agree on facts, circumstances, or interpretation.

Where different versions of the same event came from is a kind of mystery. Underlying causes and biases may be subtle and difficult to identify. Questions about motives may be raised. This may be referred to as phenomenological: an event or phenomenon may be experienced very differently depending on observers' subjective experiences. As the saying goes, "one man's meat is another man's poison."

A creative teacher can take advantage of the phenomenological effect by studying a subject through contrasting or competing lenses. Teachers can promote discussions about "agendas," how viewpoints invade everything from science to films to news reports (Phye 2001).

What different theorists or critics consider art could be the basis for a discussion of point of view. Students may argue about the form and function of art, its purpose and construction. Such clashes promote the consideration of multiple perspectives and may be used to broaden students' ideas about art. A variety of theoretical and critical viewpoints may be used to enrich these definitions.

History, like art, is a subject replete with disputes over facts, interpretations, and theories. There are many stimulating ways to compare and contrast "great men" (what, no women?) or theories of individual heroes versus "social movements." Students enjoy arguing over which facts bolster one side or the other, trying to understand the contrasting viewpoints.

As students foray into interpretations of viewpoints, they tend to be less accepting of one view as "right." Identifying agendas and hidden messages becomes part of the play. Learners are encouraged to grow more critical of current arguments.

Understanding the reasons behind differing views, checking out which have the best support, is excellent training for real life. Interpreting and synthesizing viewpoints also promotes valuable insights into checking perspectives against evidence and evaluating viewpoints.

COMPLEMENTARY, CONFUSING, AND CLASHING PERSPECTIVES

Perspectives may complement each other by providing different accounts. Views may be clear or confusing. They may also clash head-on, presenting diametrically opposed ideologies or philosophies (Ainsworth 2006).

Creative teachers should examine a topic to decide what opportunities are presented by the viewpoints expressed, for example:

a. a range of views (e.g., the auto accident),
b. overlapping sets (e.g., what is, or isn't, art),
c. antagonistic sides (e.g., liberal and conservative political views).

Make sure that the viewpoints are balanced and representative, as well as understandable.

Perspectives do not always fall into neat and easily arranged sets. Views most often range across a continuum of perceptions that share some features and differ on others. Therefore, students must be taught a comparative approach to evaluate perspectives.

Even clashing views may contain overlapping information, although it is used to reach very different conclusions. This confusing situation reflects the realities of human experience, and is precisely what makes the study of perspectives so challenging yet so rewarding (Weitzman and Weitzman 2000). We begin to understand "where people are coming from" and why views differ and evolve. Students and teachers identify a big picture of views across an issue or topic.

SEEKING TRUTH FROM MULTIPLE VIEWPOINTS: BIAS, PERCEPTION, AND "POSITIONALITY"

Bias is built into perspective. Prejudice or bias isn't necessarily a moral issue and often develops from experience. People may be unaware of underlying subjectivity, bias, or prejudice.

Rather than viewing bias as a potential danger (a viewpoint on viewpoints), creative teachers should take advantage of it. By enabling students to identify and understand bias, creative teachers are helping them to understand the life experiences and theories that shape our views.

Bias may simply grow out of a situation. This is often called "positionality." What you experience is determined by your position, where you are, a kind of lateral thinking (De Bono 1977). For example, a British soldier at Bunker Hill at the beginning of the American Revolution would very likely have a different perspective from that of a colonial patriot, let alone a foreign visitor.

Bias may also arise from a person's perception of events, often based on previous experiences. A birdwatcher, for instance, might notice birds in a tree in a much more detailed way than would a casual observer or uninterested passerby. Urban folk may overlook creatures of the wild entirely. A perspective in this case is a type of orientation based on previous knowledge, memory, and interests.

Finally, bias may arise from a well-developed philosophical or ideological belief. A deeply religious person, or someone with strong political convictions, has a predetermined point of view that influences perceptions on topics dear to them. A news item, perhaps about the president of the US, might lead to quite different interpretations and value judgments depending on the reader's political beliefs.

Settings, roles, social mores, and the "temper of the times" influence how we view certain subjects and issues, sometimes quite strongly. Many seventeenth- and eighteenth-century explorers had very biased—racist—views of the people they encountered. These ideas arose from their culture, perhaps as justification for conquest, or simply to reinforce superior views of themselves. Often they arose out of ignorance, an inability to understand people and customs that were different. This is referred to as ethnocentrism. Today, most of us try to be more sensitive to such racial and ethnic bias, although it certainly exists in many contemporary resources, including textbooks.

Social science theory and research on human differences, both biological and social, enable teachers to arouse consciousness of biases. Some subjects can help students control for bias, giving them the opportunity to develop a more accurate, "truthful" overview of perspectives. Thus, students learn to identify bias in terms of positionality, perspective, and ideology.

Trying to harmonize viewpoints offers students insights into why differences develop and how they may be resolved. Students are better able to understand and explain the origins and underlying rationale for bias. Participants have a new grasp of disputes, perspectives, biases, and competing or conflicting views as part of the human predicament. And they may learn that sometimes we cannot, or should not, decide prematurely.

From this aerial position, creative teachers can fly above the many competing views.

PUZZLEMENT AND PARTICIPATION

Puzzlement, perplexity, and viewpoint are engines that strongly share a sense of mystery. Each focuses on contested accounts that are open to more than one interpretation. There are no definitive answers to questions involving evidence subject to more than one interpretation. They require detective work to understand and evaluate alternative explanations and solutions.

The many complexities of mystery and perspective therefore support a range of higher-order inquiry skills, especially inference, corroboration, and synthesis (Weisberg 1988). Participation usually burgeons during a mystery or POV lesson because intrinsically interesting problems engage students. They may, in fact, take control of the materials to promote and discuss their own hypotheses.

Some students will want to express their views, while others will be determined to resolve the problem. As this type of lesson picks up speed, students will begin a dialogue with the content, the teacher, and each other. A creative teacher supports and sustains this process in three ways:

first, by rewarding conversation and discussion;

second, by guiding students toward the unsolved and unexplained features of the content; and

third, by designing lessons that challenge thinking while providing just enough answers and ideas to limit frustration.

Puzzlement and perplexity foster problem-solving. Point of view widens the range of students' perception, fostering comparison, contrast, and eventually

---

TEXTBOX 9.1

AN OUT-OF-THE-BOX LESSON

Write your own version of an event from at least two perspectives. You can write one as a witness or an insider. Then write the second from an entirely different angle, that of an outsider or perhaps as a poet or historian, maybe that of a blind person.

■

---

an overview of competing interpretations. Students understand the origins and evolution of competing "agendas," theories, and positions.

Ultimately, students will begin to evaluate the explanatory power of competing interpretations or theories.

Adjudicating Perspectives

By adjudicating perspectives, by solving mysteries, even if there are only tentative conclusions, students are learning to be creative. They are developing a set of skills and meta-cognitive approaches to identifying and solving problems. They are learning to identify bias by closely examining different perspectives as well as the spectrum of views on a given topic. With practice, students will need less and less direction and guidance. As independent learners, they can face new and challenging problems with highly developed skills.

Once learners work through several mysteries, collating and testing evidence against explanations and hypotheses, they begin to acquire methods of investigation, habits of mind that fit the demands of their subject. They can then evaluate which perspective, or which combination of views, appears best supported by the overall evidence and can defend their conclusion in public. Students gain a feeling of satisfaction and fascination along affective/emotional lines, as well as a sense of accomplishment.

Once outside the box, students can look back inside if they wish, or begin to develop ideas that bounce off the walls. They may invent new ideas about perspective and test these against data they research and select, from feelings of affection as much as any pragmatic purpose. Perhaps students are on the threshold of invention and innovation in a subject that has captured and sustained their interest. They have become conscious of areas of inquiry that will interest and motivate them for years to come. A wonder!

CONCLUSION

Mystery and point of view are two of the most challenging yet rewarding complex strategies or engines for creative problem-solving and teaching (Sternberg and Frensch 1999). Both require a good deal of teacher planning and curriculum design, yielding content that is restructured to stimulate higher-order cognition and affect.

Students take up the role of detectives, going beyond the data given to create theories that explain who, how, when, where, and why. They bolster their investigative skills using strategies developed earlier, such as close observation, definition, and analogy. They use new skills, such as corroboration and resolution, to examine and compare perspectives.

Resolution of conflicts and multiple viewpoints are tested against research. However, caution is advised. No matter how satisfied students may be with their hard-won conclusions, creative learning demands that interpretations be open to constant revision. Cases can be reopened as needed. Old files should be reviewed in light of new findings and new information.

For example, the deepest mysteries of human evolution change constantly as new, often surprising, discoveries are made. Perhaps cave folk in southern France really didn't invent painting. Recently, in a cave in South Africa, paint mixes dating back 100,000 years were found, from beings who might not fit the definition (perhaps rigid) of *Homo sapiens*. Our ancestors were perhaps a good deal further along than we (ethnocentric beings) have imagined.

So these new clues demand a reinterpretation of prevailing conclusions! Perhaps we need to re-examine the points of view of researchers and archeologists in the field, checking their assumptions against the latest discoveries. Creative interpretation can lead to out-of-the-box and off-the-wall inferences about beings (maybe human) and their capabilities at very early times. Teachers can design lessons to enhance and encourage problem-finding and -solving using perspectives (Jonassen 2000).

Maybe it is time for artistic, literary, and scientific re-interpretations of human capabilities that we may underrate in schools (Simon 1973). So let us

---

TEXTBOX 9.2

BONUS BOX LESSON

Go back to the painting that opens this chapter and take another look.

1. Why does the artist, Hogarth, in his painting *False Perspectives*, imply that lack of perspective leads to "absurdities?" What does he mean by absurdity?
2. How does an artist give you "perspective?" How does an artist create three dimensions, or only two, or just one? What is the purpose of perspective in art, and how does it compare to perspective in literature or history?
3. Is there perspective in maps, too? Does a map really look like the earth? Why or why not?
4. Is it possible to achieve peace in diplomacy or disputes if you only have one perspective?

---

provide new and improved opportunities in this, the Age of Testing, and the dawning Age of Common Core Standards, the Aquarius of the Internet.

Let's surmount the contradictions of perspective to spark a new sense of creativity in the land.

Building mysteries and presenting viewpoints in our classrooms expands the breadth and depth of learning. Knowledge takes on new meaning. More importantly, we take charge of our own procedures for making sense of perspective. Disagreement and difference fascinate rather than frighten us and we take competing and clashing perspectives in our stride. We are outside the box of controlled and controlling monochromatic solutions.

Creative teachers and learners are comfortable with the challenges of uncertainty and ambiguity, and the process of making sense of different and differing perspectives.

REFERENCES

Ainsworth, S. E. 2006. "DeFT: A Conceptual Framework for Learning with Multiple Representations." *Learning and Instruction* 16 (3): 183–98.

Averchenko, A. 1984. "Point of View." In *Social Work Processes*, 3rd ed., edited by B. Compton and B. Galaxy, 302–3. Homewood, IL: Dorsey Press.

De Bono, E. 1977. *Lateral Thinking: A Textbook of Creativity*. New York: Penguin Books.

Doyle, L., ed. 2001. *Bodies of Resistance: New Phenomenologies of Politics, Agency, and Culture*. Evanston, IL: Northwestern University Press.

Gallagher, S., and D. Zahavi. 2007. *The Phenomenological Mind*. London: Routledge.

Jonassen, D. H. 2000. "Toward a Design Theory of Problem Solving." *Educational Technology: Research and Development* 48 (4): 63–85.

Mumon. 1228 (1934). *The Gateless Gate*. Translated by Nyogen Senzaki and Paul Reps. A collection of Zen koans/Wikipedia.

Paulson, R. 1965. *Hogarth's Graphic Works*. New Haven: Yale University Press.

Perkins, D. 2000. *Archimedes' Bathtub: The Art and Logic of Breakthrough Thinking*. New York: W.W. Norton.

Phye, G. D. 2001. "Problem-Solving Instruction and Problem Solving Transfer: The Correspondence Issue." *Educational Psychologist* 93:571–98.

Simon, H. A. 1973. "The Structure of Ill-Structured Problems." *Artificial Intelligence* 4 (3): 181–201.

Sternberg, R. J., and P. A. Frensch, eds. 1999. *Complex Problem Solving: Principles and Mechanisms*. Hillsdale, NJ: Erlbaum.

Weisberg, R. W. 1988. "Problem Solving and Creativity." In *The Nature of Creativity: 76 Contemporary Psychological Perspectives*, edited by Robert J. Sternberg, 148–76. Cambridge, UK: Cambridge University Press.

Weitzman, E. A., and P. Flynn Weitzman. 2000. "Problem Solving and Decision Making in Conflict Resolution." In *The Handbook of Conflict Resolution*, edited by Morton Deutsch and Peter Coleman, 185–209. San Francisco: Jossey-Bass.

10

Judgments Provoked

Apathy to Empathy, Assessment to Commitment, and Evaluation to Moral Choice

---

"Have you learned lessons only of
those who admired you, and were tender
with you, and stood aside for you?
Have you not learned great lessons
from those who rejected you, and braced
themselves against you, and disputed the
passage with you?"

—Walt Whitman, 1860

"As you go on in life, cultivating this quality of empathy will become harder, not easier. There's no community service requirement in the real world; no one forcing you to care. You'll be free to live in neighborhoods with people who are exactly like yourself, and send your kids to the same schools, and narrow your concerns to what's going on in your own little circle.

Not only that—we live in a culture that discourages empathy. A culture that too often tells us our principal goal in life is to be rich, thin, young, famous, safe, and entertained. A culture where those in power too often encourage these selfish impulses. They will tell you that the Americans who sleep in the streets and beg for food got there because they're all lazy or weak of spirit. That the inner city children who are trapped in dilapidated schools can't learn and won't learn . . . so we should just give up on them entirely. That the innocent people being slaughtered and expelled from their homes half a world away are somebody else's problem. . . .

I hope you don't listen to this. I hope you choose to broaden, and not contract, your ambit of concern. Not because you have an obligation to those who are less fortunate, although you do have that obligation. Not because you have a debt to all of those who helped you get to where you are, although you do have that debt.

It's because you have an obligation to yourself. Because our individual salvation depends on collective salvation."

—Barack Obama, Northwestern University Commencement Address, June 16, 2006

INTRODUCTION: CONVENTIONAL JUDGMENT AND MORAL/ETHICAL JUDGMENT

Creative teachers use the engine of judgment to invite and provoke assessments and ethical decisions informed by reasons and evidence (Salovey and Sluyter 1997).

In schools, analysis and evaluation are going on at almost every level, every day. Teachers are continuously assessing student behavior. Students are assessing teachers, as well as the contributions of the administration, school board, and city, state, and national agencies. Each and all assessing everybody but not themselves!

Judgment is a widely used and generally confused concept. For our purposes, it will be defined as reasoned and ethical choice involving decision-making, assessment, and evaluation, fostering higher-level thinking in the affective realm. Judgment is part and parcel of the human condition (Mayer et al. 2001).

Evaluative and ethical decision-making is provoked by questions that call for choices, ratings, criteria, and the defense of moral values. Judgments come in many forms, but should not be confused with "mere" opinions, gut reactions, or personal emotions. Creative teachers respect students' opinions, but ask learners to provide explanations and evidence for their choices.

Opinions are fine but count for a great deal less than judgments, a higher level of "emotional intelligence" (Bradberry and Greaves 2009). Argument and evaluation are part of creative pedagogy, the benefit arising from the degree and kind of research and reasoning process used in reaching conclusions.

Conventional Assessments

Decision-making   Moral/Ethical Judgments

FIGURE 10.1

While low-level affect may be valuable in classroom discussion by giving a teacher insight into students' underlying values, judgments require higher-level research and a rationale. Students learn to create rationales beginning with ratings and rankings, making decisions about what auto is best, the top football team, or the most effective diet plan. Ratings and rankings generally do not involve strong emotions, although many consumer and sports fans can exhibit intense loyalty.

Moral judgment is also concerned with choice, but the argument is grounded in philosophy and values (Haan et al. 1985). Students must recognize their own values and defend them in a way that passes muster in public. This defense helps students sharpen or soften their views based on "real-world" evidence and peer feedback.

A moral choice may involve a strong emotional component based on deep-seated beliefs, attachments, and perspectives. In fact, considerable research suggests that people usually react immediately and emotionally to a sensitive issue (Goleman 1998). It is the creative teacher's role to assist in reviewing and testing moral views as personal and public standards of conduct. Thus, while conventional choice is important, moral choice guides overall decision-making.

While conventional and moral judgments both involve decisions, these are usually about different issues. The conventional entails evaluating products, techniques, and procedures while the moral concerns public policy and personal philosophy. The moral often tends toward ideological and political considerations that shape lifestyles and exert strong influences on others.

The conventional and the moral may meet on a sliding scale of criteria and values. Complex issues, such as health care reform, assessment of teachers, or "just" warfare, require research, criteria, and moral choices. A sincere effort to study these issues would require considerable work, comparison of views, and argument before making a moral choice that is defensible.

Although moral issues are more powerful, conventional assessment can be very enlightening as well. Even something as simple as setting up criteria for buying bottled water raises many higher-order questions about price, waste, content, purity, and environmental impact. However, light usually outshines heat in deciding rating issues.

Moral or ethical judgments tend to be more exciting and enlightening, but sometimes upsetting emotionally. War as public policy can raise issues of patriotism and homicide, and efficiency and effectiveness (winning hearts and minds), as well as provoke deep revulsion for killing or a fervent embrace of nationalism. Distinguishing between substantive argument and feelings, hard data and government policy, and ideology and rationale produces long and heated exchanges without firm conclusions.

Moral judgments elicit and sustain controversies and debates as students seek to develop philosophical stands on good and evil, just and unjust. Ethical and moral debate is creative in the sense that it forces students to examine their underlying beliefs and principles. Learners hone a sense of themselves and their values. Conversations with those who hold other views build a sense of alternative or competing beliefs leading to greater openness, increased tolerance, and social networking (Kidder 1995). Creative teachers help learners refine opinions and control emotions while simultaneously taking into account the views of "others."

ADVANTAGES AND DISADVANTAGES OF PROVOKING JUDGMENT

There are numerous advantages in provoking judgments, most importantly the examination of values and value systems.

At the lowest level, a lesson involving conventional judgment, assessments of products and methods, fosters critical thinking about consumer choices. Engaged learners also become comfortable with reviewing techniques, plans, assumptions, and other aspects of the material world. In effect, the result is better consumers and producers.

Political choice is perhaps a link between conventional decisions and moral judgments. Selecting a candidate involves many criteria: personal, social, ideological, and circumstantial. Voting on issues, laws, and candidates is an opportunity to make and defend judgments. Judgments can work both ways, with values projected on candidates by voters and on voters by candidates.

Thus, moral and ethical argument is training for democratic values of debate: sharing news and views, and building tolerance for the unfamiliar, unexamined, and antagonistic. Students eventually develop a broader perspective on the range of values surrounding a given issue and begin to understand "outsider" emotions and arguments.

Open-mindedness represents progress for those familiar only with "insider" perspectives afforded by cultural values and beliefs. Empathy is an advance over openness, leading to the possibility of sympathy, a change or modification of value positions. At the very least there is feeling toward the "other" as a human being with genuine viewpoints.

Although judgments may begin with rough opinions and choices, these evolve into expressions of values supported by evidence and a rationale. Creative pedagogy seeks to legitimate discussion about the formation of values that guide decision-making. This is not simply about academic classroom analysis, but about allowing students to build views as knowledgeable and caring citizens.

Judgment also involves achieving a high level of cognitive and affective reasoning (Gardner 1983). Encountering difficult and sometimes annoying issues is excellent practice for engaging with the real world. Marking out a position that satisfies and can be defended is a way of building an identity and a philosophy based on examined values. Values are defined, analyzed, synthesized, and adopted within a classroom setting committed to treating others' views with respect and empathy. Range and depth of insight into any subject contributes to a richer, more tolerant grasp of underlying beliefs and the logic behind different, sometimes disturbing, positions.

While judgment is a powerful engine for encouraging discussion and choice, there are also many disadvantages, even difficulties, when examining morality—in or out of the classroom. Students may become confused or overwhelmed by the number of choices available. Or they may see opposing views as threatening long-held values.

As an example of the latter, students with fundamentalist beliefs may reject the idea of evolution out of hand, seeing it as contradicting the biblical narrative. Nonetheless, many fields of pedagogy advocate decision-making, choice, ethical debate, and issues-centered curricula as central to their missions (Elliott 2007).

Engaging students in issues is a great deal more difficult than involving them in the lower levels of creative thinking. Hence many teachers' unwillingness to take on controversy (Hess 2009), especially in light of the deep psychological and philosophical problems involved. No matter how neutral or open-minded, all human beings hold some beliefs that are near and dear to their hearts. These beliefs jump to the surface when people are faced with challenging conventional or ethical choices. Communities and classrooms build and reinforce values, social, religious, and political. These values may foster a sense of openness and innovation, or tradition and conformity. Most are a mix of values and beliefs, depending on the topic or issue.

Learners absorb parental and community values, allowing them greater or lesser flexibility in discussing either conventional or moral issues (Pratt et al. 1999). The higher the level of conformity in a community, the less a teacher can achieve in fostering judgments. People tend to change the beliefs and values they grew up with only under specific circumstances. They may change when they see a benefit from a new position, when circumstances dictate a change, or through education. Thus, challenging students' beliefs head-on, even when a teacher thinks they are dead wrong, is not to be undertaken lightly.

Head-on collisions may damage classroom relations and work to strengthen beliefs, not modify them. Thus, teachers need to approach judgments carefully, even if only product evaluations. Learners may be upset to find, for example, that beloved soft drinks are valueless sugar, addictive as well as fattening.

They may be upset to discover that plastic bottles are a major source of pollution, and maybe a waste of money as well. Breaking students' habits or traditions must be approached with delicacy by indirect means because of emotional attachments. A "neutral" *Consumer Reports*-type of investigation of sodas or bottled water involves group effort and rewards criteria and results. No one brand or person is singled out, with findings available to all as a basis for making new choices.

People tend to jump to conclusions based on immediate confrontation with others or with phenomena. Only later do they resort to "thinking it over," and become attentive to an observation, a problem, or an issue (Kahneman 2011). "Thus, the oft-used phrase 'pay attention' is apt: you dispose of a limited budget of attention that you can allocate . . . if you try to go beyond your budget you will fail. It is the mark of effortful activities that they interfere with each other, which is why it is difficult . . . to conduct several at once" (Kahneman 2011, 23–25).

People jump to conclusions, making instant judgments, often based on underlying emotions. These conclusions may appear satisfactory at first but are often based on misperceptions. Quick judgment and slow evaluation clash, jumbling together decisions and emotions. Characteristics of human thinking render judgment-making more difficult than observation or reasoning.

However, our goals for creative teaching and learning demand a switch from automatic acceptance of judgments to effortful ways of thinking independently and originally.

Provoking Judgments as Assessments, Evaluations, and Ethical Decisions

Judgment requires a synthesis of data, definitions, and reasons as steps toward forming a conclusion about value and choice. What is top quality, good or bad, better or best, right or wrong, or morally defensible or reprehensible is at the heart of judgment.

Both forms of judgment, conventional and moral, demand a good deal of study and thinking. However, outcomes can vary enormously in terms of depth of feeling and emotional attachment. Some students may care very strongly about the kind of car they are driving, while others see this in utilitarian terms.

Some may be revolted by military mistakes like killing civilians, or "friendly fire," while others view these deaths as being within the acceptable rules of warfare. Pacifists consider warfare totally immoral under any and all circumstances. Others may see battle as a test of heroism, an opportunity to be a warrior for one's nation. Value orientations, ideology, and religion, as well as historical context and experience, all supply adrenaline to judgments.

Because emotions are involved, judgments may explode before criteria are agreed upon, and discussion may disintegrate into disagreement. Because of the complexity of judgments, and the potential for emotional outbursts, many, if not most, teachers are chary of tackling these levels of discourse (Hess 2009).

Judgment represents teaching toward a high level of thinking, feeling, and action. Complex rationales are based on information with which students have a lesser or greater degree of emotional involvement.

Creative teachers use judgment as a means of approaching critical questions that demand rating, ranking, or ethical considerations. Emotions are used to drive discussion and a sense of caring and commitment to a developing position. Legitimating classroom discussion of controversial issues allows students to become comfortable making claims. Opinions, while important, are scrutinized in an atmosphere of argument and defensibility (Hess 2004). The result is more than a simple opinion about likes and dislikes.

From a settled, conformist point of view, keeping a distance from emotional issues seems to provide peace and contentment in classrooms, at least for the teacher. However, avoiding judgments raises questions about whether schools are fulfilling their obligation to prepare students for life in a democratic society, a life filled with decisions.

Why do teachers value peace and contentment in the classroom? Do we want to be able to stuff students full of well-adjusted knowledge that does little or nothing to expand their repertory of thinking? Don't we hope to introduce them to the real world of disagreements and debates? As noted several times in this book, ambiguity and confusion, debate and discussion, promote higher-order thinking because questions are open. Solved problems and single "right" positions do not require deliberation because conclusions are fixed. Classroom time spent deciding preferences and philosophical commitments leads to more creative ideas and greater respect for the views of others.

Students who openly express frustration or admit to their views being a "mess," are most probably a great deal more honest than those who simply agree with whatever is said or keep their thoughts to themselves (Overton 1990). Students who admit to being disturbed about difficult issues are showing progress, willing to reflect but not yet ready to commit. Creative teachers and learners cannot grow without experiencing disorientation and disturbance. Shaking up ideas is an opening to thinking outside the box. Judgments are not simply opinions or preferences, like choosing chocolate ice cream rather than vanilla, but deeply held beliefs and moral commitments. Human beings, particularly the young, need time to find values that are satisfying and represent their "true" beliefs.

Although this may seem odd, disequilibrium, loss of bearings, and other signs of confusion are necessary for learners to move on to new, higher levels of thinking (Johnson and Johnson 1997). Conformity is comforting but results in nesting wholly within the box. The outside world is avoided, new theories spurned, and moral conflicts kept at a distance. There are no disturbances, no reconsiderations of views and values. Life is easy. But not much that is new is being learned. Challenges are few, and the others' positions are not taken seriously. If no alternatives are explored, your own position isn't serious either, merely reproductive.

A creative teacher can use judgment problems, inconsistencies, and emotional issues to stimulate deep and sometimes disturbing thinking. Moral judgments are expressions of internalized emotions that are part of character and culture. Students who form judgments should be greatly appreciated for their contributions to higher-order thinking. Teachers can use assessments and moral views as powerful motivators for discussion precisely because evaluation and ethical judgment are mother lodes of definition, debate, and disagreement. Sparks may fly because thinking springs from conversations about choices.

Everyone is called upon to make decisions every day, and creative choices often solve problems more effectively than standard approaches. Using this engine, students learn to form and defend both assessments and moral judgments through legitimized debate and argument. Challenges help move students away from apathy or inattention to empathy and decision-making (Hoffman 2000). The process begins with simple opinions, proceeds to comparisons, and finally engages moral and ethical questions. Making choices, defending ethics, is training for life.

SIMPLE JUDGMENT: ASSESS EFFECTIVENESS/VALUES/ OUTPUTS/EFFICACY/VIABILITY

Simple judgments involve everyday decisions such as the best product to buy, the best way to hit a ball.

Toasters are ubiquitous but differ in color, features, style, and price. Some toast big fat slices, others only thin, two slices or four, while a few seem capable of virtually broiling a loaf of bread whole. Prices vary considerably: the giant glossy steel toaster that performs a variety of tasks costs ten times more than the ordinary little two-slice model that only toasts bread. Thus we have a problem of assessment before us.

While this is not a very vital decision, it does illustrate that however large or small, an evaluation requires data, criteria, review, and finally, a choice, even for a toaster. The same process can be applied to far more difficult choices like homes, lifestyles, autos, careers, or insurance.

Assessment is generally not very emotional, but rather businesslike and systematic. One key is collecting information on the entire range of products in a given category and organizing them for easier comparison. The process can also involve concepts, for example, deciding just what is "authentic" pizza—thick or thin crust, deep-dish, lots of toppings or merely cheese, square or round.

A second key is setting up a list of criteria for judgment. Rubrics, measures, tests, and thresholds are criteria by which to measure a product or category. The criteria may themselves be subjected to judgment and give rise to heated discussions of fairness and viability. Do we judge that toaster merely by the color of the toast it produces? Or do we add defrosting, ability to toast thick and thin slices, the sounds it makes, and other features to the list? How important is price? Do we want something made in the USA or do we not care? Yet another choice!

In-the-Box Lesson

Bottled water is convenient to carry and usually a safe, reliable product. Water is cheap, but price may vary greatly depending on where it's bought and the quantity, ranging from a quarter up to several dollars, often for the same brand in the same size bottle. There are also problems with waste disposal. Most people throw empty bottles away. A large number of these bottles, usually plastic, wind up as garbage, clogging refuse containers and drains.

Questions:

1. Why do people buy bottled water?
2. What are the advantages of bottled water for consumers?
3. What are the disadvantages for consumers?
4. Would you reuse your bottles to save money or buy new ones each time? Why?

Out-of-the-Box Lesson

Let's take a look at the eight or ten most popular brands of bottled water. Include a bottle of your own. In this experiment we will check each sample of water for a number of features, OK? These include: cost, amount, source, location of purchase or use, taste, estimate of freshness, quality of bottle (strength, ease of opening, and design), disposability, and brand name identification. Conduct your investigation in groups of three to five and make a checklist for results. Be ready to share your findings with other groups. If data are missing, note this on your final evaluation.

Extra credit is given for buyer recommendations. Include your judgment concerning branded bottled water versus tap water in a personal container of choice.

Questions:

1. How many bottled waters and tap waters did you test?
2. Could you find the origin of each, the source? Why or why not?
3. Were prices the same or did they vary? By how much? Can you find a reason for different prices?
4. Which bottles were most or least attractive? Why? Were the bottles disposable/degradable or was this left unmentioned?
5. Could you tell if the water was fresh? Did it have a taste or lack of taste? Should water have a taste? Why or why not?
6. What is "pure" water? What is "clean" water? What is "fresh" water?

7. What is your group's overall judgment on the best water? Why?
8. Based on your findings, would you recommend that bottled water is worth the cost, or that tap water is as good or better? Please explain.

Off-the-Walls Lesson

Water is necessary for human life. The human body is mainly composed of water. Most people cannot live for more than a few days without water. In many places water is readily available cheaply, while in other places, water is scarce and costly. In many cultures, geographic locations, and countries, people drink bottled water regularly because of health, convenience, and/or cost. In some countries, there is plenty of clean water available but people still drink bottled water. These bottles may be saved, reused, thrown away, crushed, or recycled.

Questions:

1. Does it matter how much water people drink?
2. Why are some countries endowed with great amounts of potable water, others not?
3. Where does water come from: rivers, seas, lakes, springs, or other sources?
4. If we buy bottled water, how do we know its origin, its value, and its real cost?
5. What is the real cost of water used in homes, offices, and personally? Is this easy or difficult to find out? Why?
6. Around the world, which countries have the cleanest, best water, and which the worst? Why?
7. Would you recommend bottled water for everyone, for no one, or for some? Why?
8. Do you buy brand name bottled water? Do you regularly reuse the bottles? Why or why not?
9. What would be the worldwide effect of people throwing away bottles, plastic and/or glass?
10. If you had to advocate the most rational way of using water personally, what would that be? If you had to advocate for national or international water use, would you give the okay to bottled water or not? Why?

Moral judgment: What value should everyone follow in an ideal world?

COMPARATIVE JUDGMENT: STRATEGIC COMPARISON BASED ON REVIEW/INTERNAL CRITERIA

At a higher level, evaluation may require comparisons between and among products, ideas, and methods of inquiry. Judgment will involve more than collecting data and defining criteria. Multiple examples are needed as an epistemological framework specifying how knowledge will be gathered and evaluated (Hart 1988).

As an example, suppose we wanted to determine the best cure for a cold. First, we'd need to define a "cold." What causes it? How do its symptoms differ from other ailments such as the flu? This type of comparative assessment is fairly complex, requiring clear criteria, a good deal of laboratory work, and judgment. Assembling examples also raises questions about whether they are analogous. Methods of comparing have to be fair because bias or faulty criteria will lead to spurious, false comparisons.

As the range of related examples expands, the focus of an inquiry is refined. Terms and ideas, definitions, similarities and differences will be clarified. Comparing ideas can shed a great deal of light on how to investigate, categorize, and assess a topic. For example, the concept of war is open to considerable interpretation and debate. How is a "police action" or a "peacekeeping mission" different from a war? Is a "guerrilla war" really a war? How many "skirmishes" constitute a war? An idea like "just wars" adds many new layers of complexity and disagreement. However, defining and debating the meaning of war allows students to expand their vocabulary and compare their definitions.

Attempting to create a new synthesis is excellent mental training that promotes literacy and opens the door to examining, and perhaps accepting, alternative viewpoints. As students become used to debate, they are often more open to learning as interpretation, that is, meanings are not fixed but may change over time and with historical context.

This unsettled world of contested definitions gives teachers a great opportunity to stimulate student judgment. As making judgments grows easier with practice, it seems like a lot more fun, too, something to be encouraged rather than avoided.

Joan and Fred Have a Conversation

What judgments can we make about war?

Read the conversation below between Fred and Joan Baez, taken from a radio broadcast during the Vietnam War. Fred is pro-war for a variety of reasons, mainly defensive, while Joan is representing anti-war protesters. Joan is strongly opposed to war in general and the Vietnam War in particular. They are having a debate about war, the Vietnam War, racism, and a lot of other issues that you should notice. Read the text carefully, taking notes on the points made by each person.

Joan: Look. A general sticks a pin into a map. A week later a bunch of young boys are sweating it out in a jungle somewhere, shooting each other's arms and legs off, crying, praying and losing control of their bowels. Doesn't it seem stupid to you?

Fred: Well, you're talking about war.

Joan: Yes, I know. Doesn't it seem stupid to you?

Fred: What do you do instead, then? Turn the other cheek, I suppose.

Joan: No. Love thine enemy but confront his evil. Love thine enemy. Thou shalt not kill.

Fred: Yeah, and look what happened to him.

Joan: He grew up.

Fred: They hung him on a damn cross is what happened to him. I don't want to get hung on a damn cross.

Joan: You won't.

Fred: Huh?

Joan: I said you don't get to choose how you're going to die. Or when. You can only decide how you are going to live. Now.

Fred: Well, I'm not going to go letting everybody step all over me, that's for sure.

Joan: Jesus said, "Resist not evil." The pacifist says just the opposite. He says to resist evil with all your heart and with all your mind and body until it has been overcome.

Fred: I don't get it.

Joan: Organized nonviolent resistance. Gandhi. He organized the Indians for nonviolent resistance and waged nonviolent war against the British until he'd freed India from the British Empire. Not bad for a first try, don't you think?

Fred: Yeah, fine, but he was dealing with the British, a civilized people. We're not.

Joan: Not a civilized people?

Fred: Not dealing with a civilized people. You just try some of that stuff on the Russians.

Joan: You mean the Chinese, don't you?

Fred: Yeah, the Chinese, try it on the Chinese.

Joan: Oh, dear. War was going on long before anybody dreamed up communism. It's just the latest justification for self-righteousness. The problem isn't communism. The problem is consensus. There's a consensus out there that it's OK to kill when your government decides who to kill. If you kill inside the country, you get in trouble. If you kill outside the country, right time, right season, latest enemy, you get a medal. There are about 130 nation-states, and each of them thinks it's a swell idea to bump off all the rest because he is more important. The pacifist thinks there is only one tribe.

Three billion members. They come first. We think killing any member of the family is a dumb idea. We think there are more decent and intelligent ways of settling differences. And man had better start investigating these other possibilities because if he doesn't, then by mistake or by design, he will probably kill off the whole damn race.

Fred: It's human nature to kill. Something you can't change.

Joan: Is it? If it's natural to kill, why do men have to go into training to learn how? There's violence in human nature, but there's also decency, love, kindness. Man organizes, buys, sells, pushes violence. The nonviolent wants to organize the opposite side. That's all nonviolence is—organized love.

Fred: You're crazy.

Joan: No doubt. Would you care to tell me the rest of the world is sane? Tell me that violence has been a great success for the past five thousand years, that the world is in fine shape, that wars have brought peace, understanding, democracy, and freedom to humankind and that killing each other has created an atmosphere of trust and hope. That it's grand for one billion people to live off of the other two billion, or that even if it hadn't been smooth going all along, we are now at last beginning to see our way though to a better world for all, as soon as we get a few minor wars out of the way.

Fred: I'm doing OK.

Joan: Consider it a lucky accident.

Fred: I believe I should defend America and all that she stands for. Don't you believe in self-defense?

Joan: No, that's how the Mafia got started. A little band of people who got together to protect peasants. I'll take Gandhi's nonviolent resistance.

The Class of Nonviolence, prepared by Colman McCarthy of the Center for Teaching Peace, 4501 Van Ness Street, NW, Washington, D.C. 20016 202-537-1372

In-the-Box Lesson
Questions:

1. Why does Joan bring up "Thou shalt not kill?" Where is that quote from?
2. Why does Joan argue for "organized nonviolent resistance?"
3. Why does Fred ask "what do you do instead" of war?
4. Why does Fred argue "It's human nature to kill?"
5. Why does Joan say "you're crazy" to Fred?
6. How did you react to their arguments?
7. Whose views are most like your own?
8. Which side would you have been on if you had lived at the time, Fred's or Joan's? Why?

Out-of-the-Box Lesson
Questions:

1. Does war seem stupid or heroic to you? Do you agree with Fred or Joan? Why?
2. What does Joan mean by "love thine enemy?" Who said that? Could you love your enemy?
3. Who is civilized and who is not, according to Joan, or Fred? Do they agree or disagree and why?
4. Is it the same to kill inside a country as outside a country? Is the war the same inside or outside? Why or why not?
5. How is war part of human nature, according to Fred? How does Joan respond to this idea of violence as part of human nature?

6. Can people be peaceful, or are they just naturally warlike? Does your answer matter in real life? Would you like to go to war, win or lose? Why would you be willing to go to war? Why not?

7. When might wars be "just" and when "unjust?" Is violence successful on a personal level? How about violence among nations, between alliances, among international groups?

8. Would you agree that self-defense is a reason, a good reason, to go to war? Why?

9. Do you think people should NEVER, EVER go to war? How would you attack or defend this idea?

Off-the-Walls Lesson

Questions:

1. What is a war? Can you define it?
2. Why do people go to war? Why don't they go?
3. What is your immediate reaction to war: positive or negative or neutral? Why?
4. When you watch a war film, do you feel exhilarated or disgusted? Why?
5. Does it matter what a war is about, and who is fighting, or do you feel the same about all wars?
6. Would you support a war (and enlist) if your country's leader asked you to? Why or why not? Would the purpose of the war matter?
7. When can wars be justified, and when not? Does self-defense work for you, or patriotism, hatred, economic gain, territorial gain, or all or none of the above?
8. Is war emotional? Is violence emotional? Do you see war as part of good or bad emotions? Would you condemn and oppose war, any war, some wars, or a few wars, or applaud wars as useful and heroic? Would you like to be one of the heroes? Why or why not?
9. What might you be willing to die for: war or peace?
10. When and why do people argue over war? What kinds of times and places bring out arguments about government policy and war?
11. Overall, what is your judgment on war as moral, as effective, as defensible? What is the highest morality: warfare, just warfare, or pacifism? Can you make a decision or is the outcome difficult? Why?

PHILOSOPHICAL JUDGMENT: EXTERNAL CRITERIA/CONSCIOUS JUDGMENTS BASED ON PHILOSOPHICAL RATIONALE OR DEFINED CRITERIA

We began this chapter by helping students to formulate and validate a simple judgment and progressed to the point where they were able to compare and evaluate cases. The third and most complex stage involves developing moral and ethical judgments based on philosophical and ideological values. This stage draws judgments from external or "superior" criteria.

These external criteria include rules, theories, and moral principles developed by philosophers, religious leaders, and other authoritative or even presumably supernatural sources. They are "external" in the sense that they didn't grow out of classroom or community dialogue, but are offered as guidelines from those who already did a good deal of deep thinking and research in formulating their positions. Many of these values form ancient bedrock for morality.

These criteria usually support and draw upon powerful emotions, deep feelings about what is right and wrong. Moral judgments are raised about how human beings should treat each other in the best of all possible worlds. In effect, philosophical and religious values offer universal ideals for behavior, for family and social relationships that govern everyday interactions. Charity, assistance for the poor, is a nearly universal value that almost everyone supports. Difficulties begin with practice.

Although not always identified, external criteria usually arise from religious values and beliefs or from the work of philosophical figures whose ideas have become part of everyday culture.

For example, John Milton, the famous poet, produced one of the earliest treatises on free speech, *Areopagitica*, on the need and justification for toleration (Milton 1644). He and several other seventeenth- and eighteenth-century philosophers presented ideas about the rule of law that are now commonly accepted. Religiously inspired examples would include the Ten Commandments, the Four Pillars of Islam, and Buddha's Eightfold Noble Path. All of these rules have been interpreted and reinterpreted across many cultures and groups.

As seen in our earlier example, the Mosaic commandment "Thou shalt not kill" could serve as a springboard for controversy about warfare, just and unjust, because the commandment seems to prohibit killing without any reservations or exceptions. So if "we" all believe in this value, how can warfare be justified?

Unlike simple or even comparative examples, moral and ethical problems cover a wide range of cases and situations, across time, space, and culture. Faith and philosophy can resonate within and between different societies because of the strong views and moral values presented. Judgments must apply universally.

Philosophical and religious judgments are based on rationales for thought and action that cut across and rise above particular cases and cultures. Humanity is assumed to behave in ways that correspond to the highest moral codes. This universal appeal fuels the great power of faiths and ideologies, many having lasted for thousands of years across vast territories.

Thus external, religiously and philosophically inspired ideas can generate almost endless conversation about making right or best judgments, contrasting ideals with the problems of daily reality.

CLASHING VIEWS, PUBLIC CONTROVERSIES

Ethical judgments are most often associated with public issues: social, political, and economic. Many teachers treat issues or controversies as "two-sided" debates. However, judgments are not always "either/or" controversies and may overlap on a variety of points. Teachers may like neat arguments divided into pros and cons, but this neat division doesn't necessarily apply to public controversies. Thus, care must be taken to research and characterize the controversy to avoid reducing it to a two-sided debate.

Ideally, judgments should be suitable for panels or discussions across a range of opinion and argument. Some may need a great deal of research because of subtle nuances that demand recognition of many shades of gray before a sound choice can be made. In the classroom excerpt below, students react to the Joan/Fred conversation about "just war." Their exchanges tend to change from taking sides to questioning definitions and refining meaning, in other words, absorbing and reflecting on a variety of positions rather than direct, head-on debate.

Real Classroom Excerpts

S1: No, no, no, you misunderstand me. I am not in favor of war just to be violent!

S2: Well, you agreed with Fred that war is often necessary to settle disputes, didn't you?

S1: Yes, but not for the same reasons. I think war is nasty and horrible for guys and women, but sometimes the US has to fight to win. There's no other way.

S2: Well that is not really Joan's view, and you are not a pacifist. I am. I believe it is always wrong, always, to kill other people. Why can't we settle disputes by talking it over and compromising? Our country is pulling out of Afghanistan and Iraq after years and years of death and war, with no real victory, a total waste of life and money.

S3: Well, actually I agree with you, but I also agree with S1 that sometimes we have to go in, like what about the Nazis, huh? Didn't we have to fight to save people and ourselves?

S1: That's just the kind of example I needed. The Nazis were so evil we had to counteract them. They killed Jews, Gypsies, and conquered most of Europe, destroying people along the way. That was a necessary war, WWII!

S2: Questions, questions. I don't know really but that war could have been avoided if everyone had really settled WWI peacefully and fairly instead of depriving Germany and its allies. I'm not sure.

S4: I think we need a "just war" compromise view. I think wars can be condemned in general, like when countries just try to steal territories or have civil wars, but I still see some examples when it is morally right to fight. That is when the other side or country is doing something totally horrible, killing their own people. For instance, I think the US and Europe should save the ordinary people in Syria right now from their own leaders.

S5: Yes, we went into Bosnia, and Iraq, and other places to save people. Most people thought that was okay even if they opposed war. That is justice, I think, don't you?

S1: I think we need a discussion of justice. Just what is justice in war? War is awful once it starts and most soldiers, even the heroic, lose their sense of humanity. The enemy takes over in their minds.

S6: There are enemies in the world and we have to protect ourselves. Our soldiers protect us as a country and work to protect a lot of places in the world that would be a worse mess. They are sacrificing for us. But just wars are wars that require us to help others out, like invading Korea during the Korean War.

We saved half of the place from destruction by the other half, which is a crazy place now.

S1: Yes, Korea is a good example of a just war in my opinion.

S2: I'm still not satisfied, not at all. You are all arguing practical examples, and that's not bad. But we should still condemn war as generally unjust and horrible. And expensive. . . .

S7: I want to ask just what is the purpose of war and how any war can be just. It seems to me that once fighting starts, justice goes out the window. But that doesn't mean we should not fight ever.

S5: Right, the purpose of war can be conquest, defense, territory, money, a lot of things, and we can't always be sure of the reasons. Sometimes there are a lot of reasons.

S8: I think Joan's argument for nonviolent organized resistance is great but just won't work. People can't always decide rationally; war is the result. People may hate each other because of wrongdoing, long-run attacks, or bad decisions.

S2: OK, but that doesn't mean we can't hold to ideals about war, just wars, or being against all wars. Wars are a waste, I think, and lead to harm on all sides, innocent and guilty, that's what Joan is trying to say; it's not worth it, not even for heroes.

(Twelfth grade, social studies classroom, Chicago, IL, May 31, 2012)

Clashing views are easier to deal with than ranges of views because they lend themselves to debate, formal or informal. In the excerpt above, students spend time trying to come to grips with their reactions to the document. We all work at defining positions as much as defending positions. At first, it seems like debate will take place, but then it devolves into a reading of the Fred and Joan argument, and a start at thinking about the values that underpin each person's views.

Some students take personal stands, others remain in an investigative and reflective mode. Taking stands is quite desirable for developing judgments. As creative teachers, we actually want to avoid a "rush to judgment," a hurried and poorly thought-through position. It takes time just to read, digest, and evaluate a document as complex as the historical conversation about the Vietnam War in relation to the philosophical concept of what is "just" in conflict.

The pros and cons of building a stadium, or arguments for and against gun control may sort out neatly. But judgments that deal with deep philosophical issues, like war or sex, involve a range of views and positions. These positions may arise from circumstances, history, morality, religion, or a combination of factors.

A creative teacher who seeks to foster deep thinking about ethical problems must study the problem in considerable depth before engaging students. Adolescents in particular need exposure to differing views of a topic. The issue or problem should be matched with its most suitable format for discussion: debate, panel, groups, class, or guest speakers.

Creative teachers provide a solid base for researching issues on which students ground arguments, discuss and debate differences, and perhaps reach consensus about what is best, right, or better.

CONCLUSION: WORKING TOWARD A STAND, SYMPATHIES AND COMMITMENTS

To help learners work toward taking a stand, teachers must supply a sampling of viewpoints on an issue or problem. As an example, the full transcript of the Fred and Joan debate is included at the end of this chapter, supplemented with a selection of documents describing the nature of and justification for war.

Any views selected for discussion and debate must represent a fair and honest sample of opinion and should *not* be weighted on the side teacher favors. Each view should be chosen for clarity, sharpness, and dramatic language. Students should at first engage with views that are distinctive and oppositional. This heightens interest and provides a sense of drama and emotional engagement. As the debate or discussion evolves, more nuanced and subtle variations may be added. Eventually, an overall picture will form in the learners' minds of the range, depth, and major arguments or moral positions on a topic.

As public conversation develops, students will slowly test and promote positions they find reasonable and emotionally satisfying (Gardner 2006). Moral/ethical judgments will provoke emotion, and this should be welcomed. Learning to balance emotions with reason, viewpoint with evidence, is part of making judgments, and each contributes to the overall debate about what is right or best. Each student should be encouraged to take a stand, agreeing or

TEXTBOX 10.1

BONUS BOX LESSON: STEPPING INTO OTHERS' SHOES

"He who knows only his own side of the case knows little of that. His reasons may be good, and no one may have been able to refute them. But if he is equally unable to refute the reasons on the opposite side; if he does not so much know what they are, he has no ground for preferring either opinion."

—John Stuart Mill, *On Liberty* (1869)

1. Why does Mill say that those who only know their own side know little? Do you agree or disagree? Why?
2. Why does Mill think you should also know the other side? What does it mean to refute a judgment you don't like?
3. Do you think people hold opinions and make judgments without grounds? Or do most people have evidence and reasons for their views? Defend your opinion.
4. Is it easier to hold your own judgment without knowing any others? Is that a fair judgment and an honest one?
5. What, in your judgment, does it take to decide on an assessment or advocate for a value? What convinces you someone has made a case like the one Mill is talking about?
6. On issues like abortion, immigration, economic growth, taxes, or foreign policy, are judgments easy or difficult? Would you want to study those judgments you disagree with as well as those you agree with on these issues? On any issues? Why?
7. Do you think it is important to discuss controversial issues in the classroom? Why or why not?

disagreeing with others. Those "on the fence," undecided, or worried, should be allowed as much time as they need to develop a stand of their own.

Some students may never develop a deep commitment, and that, too, should be accepted and respected. Moral judgments are not about truth or falsity, but about seeking a philosophy or stand, a value that is defensible in public discussion.

Judgment is a sharing of ideas on the highest level, not simply voicing an opinion, but working toward values that shape a lifelong philosophy.

DOCUMENTS TO EXTEND THE DISCUSSION OF WAR

Friedrich Nietzsche, *Thus Spoke Zarathustra: A Book for Everyone and No-one [Also Sprach Zarathustra: Ein Buch für Alle und Keinen]*

WAR INDISPENSABLE

It is nothing but fanaticism and beautiful soulism to expect very much (or even, much only) from humanity when it has forgotten how to wage war. For the present we know of no other means whereby the rough energy of the camp, the deep impersonal hatred, the cold bloodedness of murder with a good conscience, the general ardour of the system in the destruction of the enemy, the proud indifference to great losses, to one's own existence and that of one's friends, the hollow, earthquake like convulsion of the soul, can be as forcibly and certainly communicated to enervated nations as is done by every great war: owing to the brooks and streams that here break forth, which, certainly, sweep stones and rubbish of all sorts along with them and destroy the meadows of delicate cultures, the mechanism in the workshops of the mind is afterwards, in favourable circumstances, rotated by new power. Culture can by no means dispense with passions, vices, and malignities. When the Romans, after having become Imperial, had grown rather tired of war, they attempted to gain new strength by beast baitings, gladiatorial combats, and Christian persecutions. The English of today, who appear on the whole to have also renounced war, adopt other means in order to generate anew those vanishing forces; namely, the dangerous exploring expeditions, sea voyages and mountaineerings, nominally undertaken for scientific purposes, but in reality to bring home surplus strength from adventures and dangers of all kinds. Many other such substitutes for war will be discovered, but perhaps precisely thereby it will become more and more obvious that such a highly cultivated and therefore necessarily enfeebled humanity as that of modern

Europe not only needs wars, but the greatest and most terrible wars, consequently occasional relapses into barbarism, lest, by the means of culture, it should lose its culture and its very existence.

Carl von Clausewitz, *On War*

Bothered and Bewildered

The War of a community—of whole Nations, and particularly of civilised Nations—always starts from a political condition, and is called forth by a political motive. It is, therefore, a political act. Now if it was a perfect, unrestrained, and absolute expression of force, as we had to deduct it from its mere conception, then the moment it is called forth by policy it would step into the place of policy, and as something quite independent of it would set it aside, and only follow its own laws, just as a mine at the moment of explosion cannot be guided into any other direction than that which has been given to it by preparatory arrangements. This is how the thing has really been viewed hitherto, whenever a want of harmony between policy and the conduct of a War has led to theoretical distinctions of the kind. But it is not so, and the idea is radically false. War in the real world, as we have already seen, is not an extreme thing which expends itself at one single discharge; it is the operation of powers which do not develop themselves completely in the same manner and in the same measure, but which at one time expand sufficiently to overcome the resistance opposed by inertia or friction, while at another they are too weak to produce an effect; it is therefore, in a certain measure, a pulsation of violent force more or less vehement, consequently making its discharges and exhausting its powers more or less quickly—in other words, conducting more or less quickly to the aim, but always lasting long enough to admit of influence being exerted on it in its course, so as to give it this or that direction, in short, to be subject to the will of a guiding intelligence. Now if we reflect that War has its root in a political object, then naturally this original motive which called it into existence should also continue the first and highest consideration in its conduct. Still, the political object is no despotic lawgiver on that account; it must accommodate itself to the nature of the means, and though changes in these means may involve modification in the political objective, the latter always retains a prior right to consideration. Policy, therefore, is interwoven with the whole action of War, and must exercise a continuous influence upon it, as far as the nature of the forces liberated by it will permit.

We see, therefore, that War is not merely a political act, but also a real political instrument, a continuation of political commerce, a carrying out of the same by other means. All beyond this which is strictly peculiar to War relates merely to the peculiar nature of the means which it uses. That the tendencies and views of policy shall not be incompatible with these means, the Art of War in general and the Commander in each particular case may demand, and this claim is truly not a trifling one. But however powerfully this may react on political views in particular cases, still it must always be regarded as only a modification of them; for the political view is the object, War is the means, and the means must always include the object in our conception.

Carl von Clausewitz, *On War*, Book I. "On the Nature of War," 1874, 1st edition of the translation. Translated from the German by Colonel J. J. Graham, Clausewitz Reference Archive

Joan Baez

What Would You Do If?

Fred: OK. So you're a pacifist. What would you do if someone were, say, attacking your grandmother?

Joan: Attacking my poor old grandmother?

Fred: Yeah, you're in a room with your grandmother and there's a guy about to attack her and you're standing there. What would you do?

Joan: I'd yell, "Three cheers for Grandma!" and leave the room.

Fred: No, seriously. Say he had a gun and he was about to shoot her. Would you shoot him first?

Joan: Do I have a gun?

Fred: Yes.

Joan: No. I'm a pacifist, I don't have a gun.

Fred: Well, I say you do.

Joan: All right. Am I a good shot?

Fred: Yes.

Joan: I'd shoot the gun out of his hand.

Fred: No, then you're not a good shot.

Joan: I'd be afraid to shoot. Might kill Grandma.

Fred: Come on, OK, look. We'll take another example. Say, you're driving a truck. You're on a narrow road with a sheer cliff on your side. There's a little girl sitting in the middle of the road. You're going too fast to stop. What would you do?

Joan: I don't know. What would you do?

Fred: I'm asking you. You're the pacifist.

Joan: Yes, I know. All right, am I in control of the truck?

Fred: Yes.

Joan: How about if I honk my horn so she can get out of the way?

Fred: She's too young to walk. And the horn doesn't work.

Joan: I swerve around to the left of her since she's not going anywhere.

Fred: No, there's been a landslide.

Joan: Oh. Well then, I would try to drive the truck over the cliff and save the little girl.

Silence

Fred: Well, say there's someone else in the truck with you. Then what?

Joan: What's my decision have to do with my being a pacifist?

Fred: There's two of you in the truck and only one little girl.

Joan: Someone once said if you have a choice between a real evil and a hypothetical evil, always take the real one.

Fred: Huh?

Joan: I said, why are you so anxious to kill off all the pacifists?

Fred: I'm not. I just want to know what you'd do if . . .

Joan: If I was in a truck with a friend driving very fast on a one-lane road approaching a dangerous impasse where a ten-month-old girl is sitting in the middle of the road with a landslide on one side of her and a sheer drop-off on the other.

Fred: That's right.

Joan: I would probably slam on the brakes, thus sending my friend through the windscreen, skid into the landslide, run over the little girl, sail off the cliff and plunge to my own death. No doubt Grandma's house would be at the bottom of the ravine and the truck would crash through her roof and blow up in her living room where she was finally being attacked for the first, and last, time.

Fred: You haven't answered my question. You're just trying to get out of it . . .

Joan: I'm really trying to say a couple of things. One is that no one knows what they'll do in a moment of crisis and hypothetical questions get hypothetical answers. I'm also hinting that you've made it impossible for me to come out of the situation without having killed one or more people. Then you say, "Pacifism is a nice idea, but it won't work." But that's not what bothers me.

Fred: What bothers you?

Joan: Well, you might not like it because it's not hypothetical. It's real. And it makes the assault on Grandma look like a garden party.

Fred: What's that?

Joan: I'm thinking about how we put people through a training process so they'll find out the really good, efficient ways of killing. Nothing incidental like trucks and landslides. Just the opposite, really. You know, how to growl and yell, kill and crawl and jump out of airplanes. Real organized stuff. Hell, you have to be able to run a bayonet through Grandma's middle.

Fred: That's something entirely different.

Joan: Sure. And don't you see it's much harder to look at, because its real, and it's going on right now? Look. A general sticks a pin into a map. A week later a bunch of young boys are sweating it out in a jungle somewhere, shooting each other's arms and legs off, crying, praying and losing control of their bowels. Doesn't it seem stupid to you?

Fred: Well, you're talking about war.

Joan: Yes, I know. Doesn't it seem stupid to you?

Fred: What do you do instead, then? Turn the other cheek, I suppose.

Joan: No. Love thine enemy but confront his evil. Love thine enemy. Thou shalt not kill.

Fred: Yeah, and look what happened to him.

Joan: He grew up.

Fred: They hung him on a damn cross is what happened to him. I don't want to get hung on a damn cross.

Joan: You won't.

Fred: Huh?

Joan: I said you don't get to choose how you're going to die. Or when. You can only decide how you are going to live. Now.

Fred: Well, I'm not going to go letting everybody step all over me, that's for sure.

Joan: Jesus said, "Resist not evil." The pacifist says just the opposite. He says to resist evil with all your heart and with all your mind and body until it has been overcome.

Fred: I don't get it.

Joan: Organized nonviolent resistance. Gandhi. He organized the Indians for nonviolent resistance and waged nonviolent war against the British until he'd freed India from the British Empire. Not bad for a first try, don't you think?

Fred: Yeah, fine, but he was dealing with the British, a civilized people. We're not.

Joan: Not a civilized people?

Fred: Not dealing with a civilized people. You just try some of that stuff on the Russians.

Joan: You mean the Chinese, don't you?

Fred: Yeah, the Chinese, try it on the Chinese.

Joan: Oh, dear. War was going on long before anybody dreamed up communism. It's just the latest justification for self-righteousness. The problem isn't communism. The problem is consensus. There's a consensus out there that it's OK to kill when your government decides who to kill. If you kill inside the country, you get in trouble. If you kill outside the country, right time, right season, latest enemy, you get a medal. There are about 130 nation-states, and each of them thinks it's a swell idea to bump off all the rest because he is more important. The pacifist thinks there is only one tribe. Three billion members. They come first. We think killing any member of the family is a dumb idea. We think there are more decent and intelligent ways of settling differences. And man had better start investigating these other possibilities because if he doesn't, then by mistake or by design, he will probably kill off the whole damn race.

Fred: It's human nature to kill. Something you can't change.

Joan: Is it? If it's natural to kill, why do men have to go into training to learn how? There's violence in human nature, but there's also decency, love, kindness. Man organizes, buys, sells, pushes violence. The nonviolent wants to organize the opposite side. That's all nonviolence is—organized love.

Fred: You're crazy.

Joan: No doubt. Would you care to tell me the rest of the world is sane? Tell me that violence has been a great success for the past five thousand years, that the world is in fine shape, that wars have brought peace, understanding, democracy, and freedom to humankind and that killing each other has created an atmosphere of trust and hope. That it's grand for one billion people to live off of the other two billion, or that even if it hadn't been smooth going all along, we are now at last beginning to see our way though to a better world for all, as soon as we get a few minor wars out of the way.

Fred: I'm doing OK.

Joan: Consider it a lucky accident.

Fred: I believe I should defend America and all that she stands for. Don't you believe in self-defense?

Joan: No, that's how the mafia got started. A little band of people who got together to protect peasants. I'll take Gandhi's nonviolent resistance.

Fred: I still don't get the point of nonviolence.

Joan: The point of nonviolence is to build a floor, a strong new floor, beneath which we can no longer sink. A platform which stands a few feet above napalm, torture, exploitation, poison gas, nuclear bombs, the works. Give man a decent place to stand. He's been wallowing around in human blood and vomit and burnt flesh, screaming how it's going to bring peace to the world. He sticks his head out of the hole for a minute and sees a bunch of people gathering together and trying to build a structure above ground in the fresh air. "Nice idea, but not very practical," he shouts and slides back into the hole. It was the same kind of thing when man found out the world was round. He fought for years to have it remain flat, with every proof on hand that it was not flat at all. It had no edge to drop off or sea monsters to swallow up his little ship in their gaping jaws.

Fred: How are you going to build this practical structure?

Joan: From the ground up. By studying, experimenting with every possible alternative to violence on every level. By learning how to say no to the nation-state, "NO" to war taxes, "NO" to military conscription, "NO" to killing in general, "YES" to co-operation, by starting new institutions which are based on the assumption that murder in any form is ruled out, by making and keeping in touch with nonviolent contacts all over the world, by engaging ourselves at every possible chance in dialogue with people, groups, to try to change the consensus that it's OK to kill.

Fred: It sounds real nice, but I just don't think it can work.

Joan: You are probably right. We probably don't have enough time. So far, we've been a glorious flop. The only thing that's been a worse flop than the organization of nonviolence has been the organization of violence.

The Class of Nonviolence, prepared by Colman McCarthy of the Center for Teaching Peace, 4501 Van Ness Street, NW, Washington, D.C. 20016 202-537-1372

Mount Holyoke College

Principles of the Just War
1. A just war can only be waged as a last resort. All non-violent options must be exhausted before the use of force can be justified.
2. A war is just only if it is waged by a legitimate authority. Even just causes cannot be served by actions taken by individuals or groups who do not constitute an authority sanctioned by whatever the society and outsiders to the society deem legitimate.
3. A just war can only be fought to redress a wrong suffered. For example, self-defense against an armed attack is always considered to be a just cause (although the justice of the cause is not sufficient—see point 4). Further, a just war can only be fought with "right" intentions: the only permissible objective of a just war is to redress the injury.

4. A war can only be just if it is fought with a reasonable chance of success. Deaths and injury incurred in a hopeless cause are not morally justifiable.
5. The ultimate goal of a just war is to re-establish peace. More specifically, the peace established after the war must be preferable to the peace that would have prevailed if the war had not been fought.
6. The violence used in the war must be proportional to the injury suffered. States are prohibited from using force not necessary to attain the limited objective of addressing the injury suffered.
7. The weapons used in war must discriminate between combatants and non-combatants. Civilians are never permissible targets of war, and every effort must be taken to avoid killing civilians. The deaths of civilians are justified only if they are unavoidable victims of a deliberate attack on a military target.

mtholyoke.edu/justwar.htm

REFERENCES

Bradberry, T., and J. Greaves. 2009. *Emotional Intelligence 2.0.* San Francisco: Publishers Group West.

Elliott, D. 2007. *Ethics in the First Person: A Guide to Teaching and Learning Practical Ethics.* Lanham, MD: Rowman and Littlefield.

Gardner, H. 1983. *Frames of Mind.* New York: Basic Books.

———. 2006. *Changing Mind: The Art and Science of Changing Our Own and Other People's Minds.* Boston: Harvard Business School Press.

Goleman, D. 1998. *Working with Emotional Intelligence.* New York: Bantam Books.

Haan, N., E. Aerts, and B. Cooper. 1985. *On Moral Grounds: The Search for Practical Morality.* New York: New York University Press.

Hart, D. 1988. "A Longitudinal Study of Adolescents' Socialization and Identification as Predictors of Adult Moral Judgment Development." *Merrill-Palmer Quarterly* 34 (3): 245–60.

Hess, D. 2004. "Controversies about Controversial Issues in Democratic Education." *Political Science and Politics* 37 (2): 257–61.

———. 2009. *Controversy in the Classroom: The Democratic Power of Discussion.* New York: Routledge.

Hoffman, M. L. 2000. *Empathy and Moral Development*. Cambridge, UK: Cambridge University Press.

Johnson, D. W., and F. P. Johnson. 1997. *Joining Together*. Boston: Allyn & Bacon.

Kahneman, D. 2011. *Thinking, Fast and Slow*. New York: Farrar, Straus and Giroux.

Kidder, R. M. 1995. *How Good People Make Tough Choices: Resolving the Dilemmas of Ethical Living*. New York: Morrow.

Mayer, J. D., P. Salovey, D. L. Caruso, and G. Sitarenios. 2001. "Emotional Intelligence as a Standard Intelligence." *Emotion* 1:232–42.

Milton, J. 1644. *Areopagitica: A Speech of John Milton*. London.

Overton, W. F., ed. 1990. *Reasoning, Necessity, and Logic: Developmental Perspectives*. Hillsdale, NJ: Erlbaum.

Pratt, M. W., J. E. Norris, M. L. Arnold, and R. Filyer. 1999. "Generativity and Moral Development as Predictors of Value-Socialization Narratives for Young Persons across the Adult Life Span: From Lessons Learned to Stories Shared." *Psychology and Aging* 14 (3): 414–26.

Salovey, P., and D. J. Sluyter, eds. 1997. *Emotional Development and Emotional Intelligence: Educational Implications*. New York: Basic Books.

The Rules and Rationale for Creativity in the Twenty-first Century and Beyond

A *"Political Economy" for Creative Classrooms*

"Without the playing with fantasy no creative work has ever yet come to birth. The debt we owe to the play of imagination is incalculable."

—Carl Jung

"**Creating**: Putting elements together to form a coherent or functional whole; reorganizing elements into a new pattern or structure through generating, planning, or producing."

—Anderson and Krathwohl 2001, pp. 67–68

INTRODUCTION

The new taxonomy for educational objectives places "create" at the very top of an inverted pyramid.

This new taxonomic pyramid is constructed to emphasize higher- rather than lower-level thinking, yet teachers persist in seeing pedagogy as recitation (Krathwohl 2002). Recitation and lecture are traditional teaching methods dating back thousands of years. While they work well in promoting some skills, like memory, they are generally ineffective in prompting creativity.

School and work experiences can be designed to build a sense of the creative without neglecting content, an idea vigorously proposed decades ago (Dewey 1938). The taxonomy can be used to design "leveled" materials, with the full cooperation of teachers who, after all, will be the delivery agents for the new curricula (Ferguson 2002).

The very meaning of creativity needs review and broadening to include "relived" as well as innovative experiences (Runco 2004). And creating can be integrated with other theories like multiple intelligences to cover broad ranges of student talent (Noble 2004).

NEW MODEL FOR BLOOM'S TAXONOMY

Creativity seems to flourish when there is a convergence of social, cultural, and educational influences that ebbs and flows with historical circumstances (Amabile 1996). On the whole, freer and more democratic societies are more likely to foster creative conditions than are controlled and authoritarian settings. At the present moment, support, in the form of policy and funding, for innovation and experimentation in the schools is critical.

Within education, creativity can be supported across large organizations, but is usually the province of teacher-student relationships. However, orga-

FIGURE 11.1

nizations that promote open access, freedom to innovate, and participation have the edge in terms of fostering creativity. In school systems this openness encourages innovation by teachers and participation by students.

In contrast, top-down management, in the form of rigid rules, tight testing programs, and mandated curricula decreases both creativity and student involvement (Amabile 1998). Emphasis on teacher professionalism bolsters independent thinking and experimentation, while prescription and direction of teachers' actions limit innovation. Criticism and mistrust, and a lack of respect, diminish the impact of all teachers. The concomitant effects on learners are inattention, disinterest, and lower scores on tests, precisely the opposite of what are demanded by authorities as signals of success.

Despite the emphasis on creativity in the business and cultural communities, within education reproduction rather than production is the norm. The trend is toward greater control, tighter standards, and more rigidity. A recent popularization of "common core" standards moves in the direction of building new approaches, but implementation across the teaching profession is many years away (National Governors Association 2010).

Let's consider the factors described in this book as expanding or inhibiting creativity to shape the "economy" of a classroom. View a classroom as having its own "knowledge and invention" economy where many "micro" and "macro" forces are at work in producing results.

Each factor works to propel or inhibit learning, particularly higher-order learning. Given that the new taxonomy we're using places creativity at the top, we, as educators, need to think outside the box to achieve quality, or remain trapped in the lower levels of remembering and, perhaps, understanding.

Supplies of information, lessons, and curriculum matched with imaginative instruction should yield greater creativity than old-fashioned materials and methods, provided proper implementation. Investment in classroom resources, just as in business, is required to promote achievement and literacy across major and minor subjects.

A POLITICAL ECONOMY OF THE CLASSROOM

Originally, a "political economy" was defined as the conditions necessary for the organization of production and consumption within states and nations (de Montchrestien 1615). In the original model, a harmonious order of political economy was thought to result in personal, social, and governmental wealth.

As a metaphor for education, it could be argued that the classroom is "home" and the school a "nation" within a larger world of trade and exchange of ideas and knowledge. Bolstering creativity enhances and stimulates productivity. Older ideas and information are rearranged, extended, and reconfigured to form new products and ideas. Rather than currency, educational wealth is represented by ideas, preferably based on evidence. Research and development are necessary to test and revise ideas to exchange or trade with others.

In most classrooms, the emphasis is on reproduction, following along with a guide and teacher: performance success defined as accurate mimicry of the input. A perfect test score on an examination of knowledge represents 100 percent success at memorization. These results, though perfect, are at the lowest levels of Bloom's cognitive, affective, and psychomotor taxonomies. Thus, teachers must invest a lot of labor to produce, at best, a marginal gain in memorization.

In all discussions of creativity, there is general agreement that an economy of the classroom (any classroom, whether in a home, school, business, church, etc.) should prioritize interpretation and imagination. The starting point is the same as it is for memorization: close scrutiny of the knowledge available. The difference is that *the learners* decide usefulness and meaning, reason, and make decisions. (They actually do so anyway!)

Learners must be active in the acquisition of knowledge from the base level all the way up to making assessments and moral judgments at the highest level. Otherwise, lack of trade and production (of ideas) will lead to stagnation and deflation. Storage of knowledge is wonderful, but may produce a false sense of comfort. The data may be saved, but it is easily overlooked or forgotten. We forget all about applying it to persisting problems and new issues.

Available knowledge should be made useful by employing skills of finding, analyzing, and evaluating sources. Such skills, actively practiced under the guidance of skillful teachers, are the most valuable resources for translating the rapidly accumulating data of the twenty-first century. Yet the majority of teachers feel, correctly in most cases, that the "system" speaks with at least two tongues. There is a strong sense that goals are schizoid, particularly to professionals who value discourse and participation (Craft 2005).

One tongue says get the knowledge scores up, cover ground, absorb and repeat text, think inside the box, copy the box, keep quiet. The other tongue says think independently, be inventive, don't plagiarize, go out of the box or even off the walls. Students, learners, children, employees, and teachers know what the real score is and if they sense conformity will get them ahead, creativity is abandoned. In contrast, creativity arises in an atmosphere where experimentation and open exchanges of ideas are valued. New ideas, new products, and reconfigurations must be welcomed to promote imagination.

Eras of great creativity usually produced considerable economic wealth and culture. Creative classrooms could also produce a wealth of ideas if teachers were encouraged to promote imagination and liberated from the yoke of oppressive reproduction (McCrae 1987). In a system sending mixed signals and fostering disrespect for teachers, the likelihood of developing rich classroom economies is rather low.

Top-down direction and higher standards based on repetition and replication, coupled with relative inattention to either methods or content, is a formula for confusion, not success. Surprisingly, just as the electronic age is providing us with wondrous technology and almost unlimited data, teachers find themselves in a dilemma. Most receive mixed signals about what to do and where to go for a new model of instruction.

Education lacks a model that utilizes the rich resources entering classroom economies, caught between competing goals and standards.

WHERE WE'RE COMING FROM . . .

How have we gotten ourselves in a box that works against creativity? The reasons are many and mostly not intentional.

First, in the age of electronics, traditions that worked in the past are losing much of their meaning as knowledge grows geometrically. What is commonly thought of as factual information is readily available in great quantities, even those portions that were once censored or suppressed. So much is available that it becomes a heavy burden and a distraction for many teachers and learners. Despite the vast amount of knowledge available, creativity may actually be suffering! Reading is seen as a chore, not a pleasure.

Databases offer huge quantities of knowledge, but relatively little in the way of navigational tools to guide meaningful thinking. Thus, twenty-first-century learning requires heuristic skills, allowing teachers and learners to identify needed information and how and where to locate it.

Second, knowledge sought requires ideas to search it out. Investigators must have at least a few clues, concepts, and sources before beginning an inquiry. Concepts are key. Clueless students often do not know where to start and thus end up imitating or copying what is available without digesting or interpreting the content. Even teachers, overwhelmed by the amount of available information and pressed for time, may resort to the source that is easily reproducible or attractive, but inauthentic.

Third, schools currently being "reformed" are actually in decline because almost all of the pressures on teachers are to produce higher test scores. The tests themselves are heavily weighted toward old-fashioned conceptions of knowledge as facts rather than as skills for sourcing, analysis, and insight. Common core standards call for literacy, not regurgitation.

Fourth, pressured teachers, evaluated teachers, much-criticized teachers, tend to fall back to the lowest common denominator of instruction: telling. Telling is part of the oldest metaphor for teaching, teaching as lecture and recitation, memorization and repetition. Alas, we are using the new sophisticated electronic compilations to reinforce traditional methods. The known is treated as far more important than the how or why to be learned.

Fifth, there is confusion about creativity and how it's achieved, coupled with reproduction of old methods using new technology. A lecture presented on a SMARTboard, using an iPad, or as a PowerPoint presentation is still a lecture. Despite electronic capabilities, the learner is not invited to be a participant in the construction of knowledge.

Sixth, despite the technology available, educational systems are often far behind. In fact, most schools, much less systems, prohibit the use of many electronics, and cutting-edge tools are often unavailable to teachers or students (Pink 2005). Curricula are largely out of sync with technology. No one takes time to review websites. And many teachers and administrators think that simply using computers will improve learning.

WHERE WE MAY BE GOING . . . PROBABLY

The twenty-first century offers new potential for creativity (Finke, Ward, and Smith 1992). This encompasses both the acquisition of knowledge and the means to utilize vast resources. Not only has the amount of available data exploded, so have applications, methods of analysis, and the possibility of drawing new connections. The Internet offers fantastic resources including audio, images, documents, and films. YouTube, for example, now provides documentary and performance footage that was once difficult and costly to find. But YouTube is blocked in many schools!

The question for teachers is how to prepare and present materials that awaken interest, arouse ideas, and stimulate investigations. Not to mention control the distractions of advertising, gaming, and social networking, or at least put them to good use. Sadly, many classrooms incorporate the latest technology, but for didactic purposes.

Creative teaching, while valuing knowledge, places greater emphasis on problem-finding and -solving approaches. Results build slowly, with consistent input from teachers, parents, and leaders (Robinson 2010).

One avenue for development is redesigning curricula as presenting problems using a combination of old and new technology. The curriculum may be reconfigured in ways that share problems and issues rather than repeat settled conclusions. A first major advance would be to invite *problem*-finding and -solving rather than *answer*-finding and -giving. This is a longstanding goal of pragmatic educational philosophy that unites play with work and lower- with higher-level thinking (Nachmanovitch 1990).

A second major advance would be to promote skills for an electronic age including locating, organizing, and evaluating sources. The new game would focus on ability to find and check the sources for a project or assignment. Ideas would drive inquiry by identifying and testing data, not simply accepting conclusions. New ideas would represent a "win" in the classroom economy.

A third major advance would be the purposeful "hybridization" of education with entertainment. Edutainment, as the new wave might be called, would use the dramatic and motivational qualities of play to drive serious inquiry about ideas, problems, and issues. While entertainment has its dangers in education (distracting and misleading), it also has its advantages in terms of attracting attention.

We're already there, anyway, so why not recognize and use it?

Even students in my own classroom, all of them teachers or teachers to be, after acknowledging my presence with a nod, return to checking their e-mail, cell phone messages, or texting. A new-style hybridized edutainment lesson might draw them away from all their distractions. The new curriculum would combine media, methods, and views challenging students to apply ideas to evidence and create a defensible explanation and judgment.

Example Lesson

A history example might look like this: a few major documents from the US Civil War come on the screen and are read aloud, then arranged by some criterion such as frequency of certain words or terms, main ideas, "hot" (inflammatory) and "cold" (neutral) language, and so on. Discussion.

Then, all of sudden, clips are shown of several Hollywood Civil War films (preferably anachronistic and overblown). Discussion: "Did the filmmakers get it right?" Zing! Talking heads come on, four Civil War historians arguing about the meaning and message of the films and the documents. No conclusion: more discussion. Teams of students are asked to give their own interpretations, their own views.

Students read two competing theories of the Civil War by social scientists, and an excerpt from a literary work. More discussion stimulated about the Civil War and its causes, but then the teacher shifts to questions of historical literacy, the big issues of trustworthiness and truthfulness, corroboration, consistency, and conflicting interpretations.

There may be a convergence of views, but there may be conflicting views.

There are requests for more data, time for research and reflection, tentative or indeterminate conclusions. We have the resources, the technology, the skills, so we can always return for another look at the problem, right?

Either way, this is a fine example of using multiple sources, encouraging critical thinking, and being part of twenty-first-century databases and a technology that integrates media, sources, and entertainment in the service of educating sharp-witted citizens of the republic. Do you agree?

Why not invent a "hybrid" lesson of your own for math, science, art, music, language?

That's what I would like to have ready for my classroom.

That's where we're probably going.

CONCLUSION

To continue in the twenty-first century and get to the twenty-second, creative instructors must change their ideas about the curriculum and instruction across subjects.

Lesson must combine and integrate text, image, and sound, entertainment sources and scholarship. Topics may be presented as fusions of fact and fiction, expert and popular views, primary and secondary sources. This would challenge students to gather facts while comparing interpretations with expert and artistic views, hypothetical or imagined.

The new push should be for "literate" consumers who are conscious of goals and sources!

Concordance and corroboration would become major skills for evolving hypotheses about the truthfulness and trustworthiness of interpretations. Learners would make their own judgments about validity and reliability. The process of decision-making across and within subjects would deepen understanding and bolster citizenship in a democratic society.

A byproduct of creative teaching and learning would be a more informed citizenry (an idea to which we often pay lip service): clever students, smarter consumers, more innovative businesspeople, and more insightful voters. We would have a population far more capable of making use of the vast knowledge resources available. And these folks would be able to distinguish junk from value, propaganda and sales pitches from verified and authenticated information.

Teachers might begin by following the steps outlined in this volume: awakening attention, arousing ideas, sparking curiosity, stimulating investigations, exploring multiple viewpoints, and provoking judgments.

Standards for creative teaching—building the reflective from the didactic, fusing tellers with askers, sparking imagination from analogy and reasoning—might be summed up by a few criteria:

Six "Uncommon Core" Performance Standards Indicative of Creative Teaching

1. Teacher talks less than half the time; students talk more than half the time.
2. A third or more of all questions posed should be higher-order (reflective and affective questions); a third or less should be lower-order (didactic and recall).
3. A quarter of the conversation, in person or online, should be student-to-student or among and between students rather than student-to-teacher or teacher-to-student.
4. Students should initiate ideas more often than the teacher does; teacher recognizes students' ideas through repetition, paraphrase, and elaboration.

5. Participation is widespread (two-thirds at least joining in), voluble, excited, and sustained (equal parts monologue, dialogue, and "multi-logue" (Zevin 2011).
6. Learners identify and check sources related to a problem.

Work and play would be fused for a richer interactive type of learning across the curriculum. Teachers would become professionals freer to innovate and experiment with their students, and stop viewing themselves as conveyors of information.

The model of instruction might finally change from its nineteenth-century industrial roots, meeting the promise of the much-touted technological "cloud" world. Factories would become think tanks for everyone.

Of course, this fantasy would happen *if* parents, students, and teachers can possibly:

- part from the nineteenth century and its contradictions of control;
- harness or neutralize the new virtual world's many distractions;
- review and revisit content as worthy and worthwhile; and
- regain respect for teachers by society and for themselves as guides and questioners.

Perhaps there can be creative teaching for everyone, in the box, out of the box, and off the walls.

REFERENCES

Amabile, T. M. 1996. *Creativity in Context.* Boulder, CO: Westview Press.

———. 1998. "How to Kill Creativity." *Harvard Business Review* 76 (5).

Anderson, L. W., and D. R. Krathwohl, eds. 2001. *A Taxonomy for Learning, Teaching and Assessing: A Revision of Bloom's Taxonomy of Educational Objectives.* Complete edition. New York: Longman.

Craft, A. 2005. *Creativity in Schools: Tensions and Dilemmas.* New York: Routledge.

De Montchrestien, A. 1615. *Traite de l'economie politique.* Paris.

Dewey, J. 1938. *Experience and Education.* New York: Collier Books.

Ferguson, C. 2002. "Using the Revised Taxonomy to Plan and Deliver Team-Taught, Integrated, Thematic Units." *Theory into Practice* 41 (4): 239–44.

Finke, R., T. B. Ward, and S. M. Smith. 1992. *Creative Cognition: Theory, Research, and Applications.* Boston: MIT Press.

Krathwohl, D. R. 2002. "A Revision of Bloom's Taxonomy: An Overview." *Theory into Practice* 41 (4): 212–18.

McCrae, R. R. 1987. "Creativity, Divergent Thinking, and Openness to Experience." *Journal of Personality and Social Psychology* 52 (6): 1258–65.

Nachmanovitch, S. 1990. *Free Play: Improvisation in Life and Art.* New York: Penguin Putnam.

National Governors Association. 2010. *Reaching Higher: The Common Core State Standards Validation Committee.* Washington, DC: NGA & CCSO.

Noble, T. 2004. "Integrating the Revised Bloom's Taxonomy with Multiple Intelligences: A Planning Tool for Curriculum Differentiation." *Teachers College Record* 106:193–98, Blackwell Publishing Limited.

Pink, D. H. 2005. *A Whole New Mind: Moving from the Information Age into the Conceptual Age.* New York: Allen & Unwin.

Robinson, A. 2010. *Sudden Genius? The Gradual Path to Creative Breakthroughs.* Oxford: Oxford University Press.

Runco, M. A. 2004. "Creativity." *Annual Review of Psychology* 55:657–87.

Zevin, J. 2011. *Teaching on a Tightrope: Diverse Roles of Great Teachers.* Lanham, MD: Rowman and Littlefield.